CONTENTS

Introduction: Kimmie Wong 1
Danielle Murphy Faris 5
Jenell Lyn Kelly 22
Hala El Khoury 36
Kristin Sullivan 53
Samantha Popp 67
Dana Peever 77
Keianna Williams 91
Brandi Kowalski 104
Diana Mantey 118
Louise Feltham 133
Micheline Edwards 147
Kathy Denise Hicks 162
Pia Prana Muggerud 176
Brooklynn Bradley-LaFleur 192
Shelley Biggs 206

INTRODUCTION

KIMMIE WONG

Hi, my name is Kimmie Wong. I am an entrepreneur, wife, and mother of three beautiful children. After being stuck in a corporate job for many years, I felt completely unfulfilled. I knew there was more to life than the normal nine-to-five grind. I had many dreams and business ideas I wanted to bring to life. Before finally stepping out of the corporate world, I had many failed attempts.

Yes, there were some days I felt hopeless and even miserable. I was unsure of what I truly wanted to dedicate my life to—I only knew I didn't want to spend it on someone else's watch. Despite many hurdles and obstacles along the way, I found my true passion as a successful publicist and marketing strategist.

Now, I am my own boss. I have the freedom to live a balanced lifestyle. Having more time to spend with my family and dedicate to the things I love has brought me so much joy and fulfillment.

Throughout my coaching career, I've spoken to many women—women who feel stuck in their daily routines while experiencing extreme pressures from society. Even though these women have incredible ideas and dreams, they just cannot seem to make those dreams come true.

There are countless strong, smart women who want to rediscover their purpose, pursue their calling, and start a business, but who face many roadblocks along the way that make them feel as if they aren't cut out for the world of entrepreneurship. Many of these women were on the verge of giving up and giving in to a life they did not really want. I resonate wholeheartedly with these women; it was as if they mirrored my own past journey.

What makes me hopeful for women's futures and their endless career opportunities? It is the fact that I've met incredible women who have endured just as much as anyone else—brave women who took the leap and the risk to follow their dreams. Some of these incredible women are featured in this book.

They share their stories with you, the women of the future, because they want to inspire you. The women in these chapters are all entrepreneurs from around the world. Even though they come from different backgrounds, the message is simple: Their powerful stories of how they brought their ideas to life will ignite the female entrepreneurs of tomorrow.

I invited these women to contribute to this book to create a powerful sense of togetherness among women. Standing as

Introduction

one, we are strong. When we collaborate, we are an unstoppable force.

If you've ever felt like your ideas aren't being heard, if the road to success seems too difficult, then these pages will show you're not alone. There are women who have walked this path before you and they all share their stories in this collective tell-all book.

This book will empower those women who have lost faith in their own abilities to continue their path—to stand back up when they've been knocked down by life's obstacles and keep pursuing their dreams. Reading their stories will reignite the fire within you and sustain you on your journey.

If they did it, so can you.

When she rises, she rises with tomorrow in mind. Even though she can't see what the future holds, she knows if she takes action now there will be a positive outcome in the future. Her ideas and dreams will manifest into reality, and it all starts with her determination to rise!

Kimmie Wong
Founder and Publisher
She Rises for Tomorrow books

Would you like to elevate your personal brand and have your message reach millions?

Visit

www.kimmiewong.com

"When our relationship with our child(ren) is strong, we can calmly and confidently conquer all parenting challenges life presents together through honor, authenticity, and purpose."

Danielle Murphy Faris

Do you ever dream of being able to offer your child a better life?

I know I did. And through an endless climb of faith, endurance, and resilience that called upon my deepest passion, skillsets both innate and acquired, and every last drop of perseverance I could muster, I was able to do just that.

It wasn't easy. The things worth having in life never are. But it shaped and defined the person I am today and the legacy I will leave for my child forever.

• • •

When my son was first born, I knew I wanted to give him a life that was beyond my capacity at the time. I was a group fitness instructor with $84,936 of student loan debt. My love for and obsession with education and personal growth had led me through a solid decade of higher and higher degrees, but not a paycheck to show for it.

My fitness instructor certification was one of the first things I pursued after high school and that, paired with my loving parents' support, served to put food in my mouth and clothes on my back for ten years of continuous training in fields such as Early Childhood Development, Psychology, Holistic Education, and Nutrition.

I was in an expensive pursuit to discover my "dream career path" and my life's purpose.

I flowed through course upon course, campus upon campus, state upon state, and even as I gave my college Valedictorian speech, or walked across the stage to accept my master's degree, my heart was empty of direction.

When I became pregnant, I immediately began to do what I did best: study! I studied books, podcasts, lectures, took classes, courses, and even reviewed my old textbooks and notes to best prepare myself for my new journey into parenthood.

The more I learned, and re-learned, the more excited I became to embark on the path of motherhood that countless other women had walked before me.

But it wasn't until the moments when I saw the words of the authors, philosophers, and theorists magically unfolding through my own child's growth and behavior before my very eyes that a realization struck my heart like a lightning bolt, and my pursuit was over.

It quickly became clear to me that I had a unique gift to understand the perspective of non-verbal infants in ways others struggled to see and knew at once that pursuing the field of early childhood development was indeed my true calling. This knack continued to unfold further later on as my ability to interact with toddlers made other adults in the room pause and commend my approach.

I had found what I was meant to do in this world.

This is how I was supposed to serve humanity.

This is the role I was destined to fulfill with my time on earth.

I was also fortunate enough to have found it during an era of abundant "mamapreneur" manifestation.

I spent a very short seven weeks basking in the dream of a brighter tomorrow, and mentally setting up my plan for my professional future during my maternity leave.

I thought up a business name, created a social media account, envisioned a website…

And I was then faced with the hard reality that I had to return to work in the fitness industry.

While my mother was a beyond wonderful grandparent babysitter in all respects, leaving my seven-week-old baby in someone else's care was just utterly nonsensical to me.

Since I was now whole-heartedly committed to using my early childhood education and becoming a professional in the field of child development, it only made sense for me to spend every moment I could being present in my own child's life.

But my financial situation did not lend itself to this notion, and I returned to my hourly position teaching group fitness classes. Every class I taught, I felt like a hollow shell of an instructor. My body language and words were playing the role on the outside, but my mind and my heart were light-years away from the studio every moment.

My soul was moving forward towards a different future, a different life, a different path, but my physical body was being stuck on another path. I was motivated to take additional (costly) trainings in the early childhood field, which meant I had to work more hours teaching fitness, and subsequently spent even *more* time away from my young son who was the spark for this entire revolution.

I was in a vicious and downward spiral, watching my dreams get further and further out of reach the harder I worked.

Something wasn't right.

As my debt and discontent grew, I worked more hours and spent less time with my family. It was always a war between sleep or posting to that old social media account I had created on a whim or adding content to that long forgotten website… and I was tired.

• • •

Then, an opportunity arose for me to become a "Master Trainer" in the fitness world where I was told I could "triple my income" and "set my own hours." Even though I knew this wasn't where I saw myself in the longer term, I believed the role would give me more time and resources to focus on starting my ultimate career path in the Early Childhood sphere.

It seemed like a necessary evil if I was ever going to escape my current rut.

So I took a gamble and spent every penny I had to haul my husband and seven-month-old baby down to a hotel in Los Angeles for seven days while I endured fourteen-hour days of grueling training, sneaking in moments of breastfeeding whenever possible.

When we got back, the role didn't pay out as promised.

I was able to "make my own hours" but it involved a great deal of unforeseen commuting which created added expenses, and even *more* time away from home yet again.

Stress, desperation, and overwhelm had become everyday feelings for me, and were manifesting into my physical health and personal relationships as well.

Exhausted, out of money, and hopeless, I was at rock bottom.

• • •

After two-and-a-half years of dreaming, learning, investing, working, fighting, and getting nowhere towards my dream career path, I began to doubt myself.

I desperately wanted to catch a break and find a way to turn things around.

Maybe I would never have the business savvy to be an entrepreneur, the tech skills to create anything, or the marketing knowledge to share my vision.

Maybe my education was wasted.

Maybe I had been foolish to have spent money on those specialty trainings that would never amount to anything.

Maybe my dream career would never be anything other than an expensive hobby...

So with a sigh of failure, I took a break from the hustle. I let the social media account dry up, the website lapse, and the vision slip away.

I put in my hours at the fitness studio, day in and day out, like a monotonous robot. I stopped fighting so hard against my current situation and spending so much energy toward discontent, and instead I made the most of the time I *did* have with my son. I focused on being present, grateful, and calm. The months passed by, and after a while I did a mental check-in with myself and discovered the dream wasn't lost completely after all.

It was still alive in the back of my heart, in a very tiny way.

I listened to one of my mentors speak about the difference between those who succeed and those who fail—those who succeeded never gave up he said. Really? I thought…*never?* What about practicality? Realism? Knowing your limits? My pragmatic side was telling me not to chase this fantasy, but my heart would never be content without at least another go around of effort.

I had to start again. But how? Where? I had very little wiggle room financially and had to play my cards carefully now. What small, practical step could I take towards the life I dreamed for myself, with minimal risk this time?

I decided to take a job where I could bring my son, working with children, so I became a nanny for the paltry sum of thirteen dollars and change per hour.

I put my digital business dream on the back burner. I simply couldn't afford it, and didn't know how to start (yet), and focused instead on gaining further experience with the practical application of my knowledge and skillset.

I was doing what genuinely interested me. I was with my own son. And I was happy.

I got to see a whole new realm of social dynamic skills emerge as my son interacted with the little girl for whom I nannied. I slowly began to pick back up where I left off with my readings.

I wasn't creating an empire, but I was no longer just a shell.

My eyes, my heart, and my mind were present, active, and ticking again.

Little did I know, the law of attraction was working behind the scenes in my favor.

• • •

And within a year, as if by chance, *something amazing happened*. I was offered a job to teach "Parent-Child" classes at an upscale private school in a different town.

We moved. I embraced this new role with every ounce of my being.

It was pure euphoria.

I shined like a ray of light each day I walked into my classroom to greet the families.

In the evenings I would bake muffins, sew puppets, type up content on various topics, and research quotes for guided discussions with the parents.

My new life had started.

My dream was now my reality.

I was finally working, living, and breathing my purpose.

My job at the school expanded and they asked me to take on even more parent-child classes. I also began to work in a group-child care setting and continued to nanny!

I was spending time with my son, bringing in money, and doing what I loved!

I was suddenly able to afford the additional trainings I had put on hold and felt I could now grow and flourish in my forever career.

I enrolled in master courses, certification programs, specialty workshops, and began studying again, which I had craved for so long.

I received several more opportunities to lead and run *other* parent-child classes, programs, and workshops from surrounding schools and organizations.

Step-by-step, I was establishing myself as a well-known local professional and walking the talk of becoming a true expert in my field with joy.

• • •

And then COVID-19 happened!

This entire new life I had poured my heart into redefining and creating for myself and my son just up and vanished within two weeks.

No more parent-child classes, group-care, or nannying. No more training courses, and no more income.

I had so much momentum building towards this dream and it all ended abruptly with a universal wave of the unknown.

I was frozen.

I knew I had to find a way to keep this field of work alive. I had come so far and now had so much education, experience, credibility, and certifications under my belt.

I had finally found my life's purpose and how I was meant serve the world—and I refused to let it go!

I remembered my mentor again and how he tried *seven* times before he got it right. What if he had given up after the second, or third? He wouldn't be where he is today.

I realized my only hope was to now circle back to the abandoned dream I had long forgotten about, to bring my parent-child work *online*.

I had no choice but to face my demon: "the tech."

Teaching live classes at the school was my scapegoat to live my dream career without having to dip a toe into the tech world. But now there was nowhere to run and nowhere to hide.

This was literally my one and only chance to continue pursuing my work in this field, where I could serve not just the families in my home community but families nationwide on a digital platform.

As I worked through even more programs and courses to learn now how to launch an online business, a recurring theme that came up was finding "*my why.*" Business coaches and gurus always want you to dig deep and find your authentic *why* for creating a business...

Through these intense trainings and mastermind groups, I realized I had a *why* that had always been in my heart, but never brought to the surface.

It wasn't just to teach parenting education and child development content.

It wasn't just so I could spend more time with my own son.

It wasn't just about serving the children (although that is a very large piece).

It was that I wanted to empower other *mothers* to identify and pursue their own dreams, with confidence that their motherhood would not suffer for it.

And that's when my business took shape.

The HAP Method is not only about parent-child education; it's a system to support a community of mothers who are striving to be their best selves for their families.

I created a structure that not only shares positive, respectful, intentional early childhood content and community with families, but also gives mothers a chance to grow, shine, and rise in *their* passion.

I know the pain of having to leave your baby for a job you dislike in order to pay the bills. I know the toll that sadness, exhaustion, and stress can have on the mother, and how that in turn, affects parenting, and parent-child relationship on the whole. I know that in order for a mother to parent in an authentic, connected, and intentional way, she must be free of inner turmoil. A mother needs sleep, peace of mind, and a sound heart in order to reap the endless benefits of a strong parent-child relationship.

By helping mothers move away from stress, and into a place of self-discovery, growth, and clarity around their parenting and personal dreams, The HAP Method delivers a truly holistic and comprehensive approach to the parent-child relationship and its subsequent impact on the well-being of both mother and child.

• • •

In closing, just making more money is not what created the better life for my child. Children don't notice or care about their family's socioeconomic status.

Children care about and thrive when they have a strong and confident role model they can count on to raise them with love, intention, and respect in a way that allows them to be true to *their* own life's calling.

And that's where my summit was reached.

I climbed up from my daily grind of stress and living pay-check-to-pay-check.

I climbed up above the heartbreak of tear-filled separations, empty and hollow work shifts, and physical and mental exhaustion.

I climbed up beyond the unhappy person I didn't want to be, and didn't want my son to see me as, to the person I am now.

I can stand tall on my mountain peak as someone who has genuinely brought value, insight, and change into the lives of countless mothers through The HAP Method. My work has benefitted the relationship of parents and young children nationwide.

That's the person I want to be for my son, and that's how I created a better life for him.

This path has allowed me to continue to share the work I love with families on a much larger scale than I could have ever imagined, set my own schedule, and most importantly, spend more time with my family.

I can now use my experience and my story to help other mothers find their drive, their voice, and their direction.

I was able to finally create the life I always dreamed of and knew was possible, but never knew how to get there.

This means I can now spend each and every day doing what I love and live the life of my dreams.

• • •

If you are a mother, who has a dream…

> I hear your heart calling for more,
> I see the spark behind your soft eyes,
> I know the tiny twinkle in the back of your mind,
> And I can feel the fire within you.

It may be small…it may be dwindling…but it's there. It's the fire that screams:

> "I want a better life for myself, my child, my family!"
> "I want to use my gifts to serve!"
> "I want to bring good to others, and let the world see my light!"

If these statements speak to you; I am with you.

I'd love to connect with you on your parenting journey so that you can excel at motherhood AND bring *your* soul's purpose to the surface.

Together, we can accomplish more on this lifelong, all-encompassing, never-ending pursuit of becoming our best selves for our families and creating the life of our dreams.

This is my story. What will yours be? I truly believe that every mother reading this already has what it takes to rise for tomorrow while writing their own story of triumph, and that journey starts today.

ABOUT THE AUTHOR

DANIELLE MURPHY FARIS

Danielle is the Founder of The HAP Method, a parent-child relationship-centered approach rooted in positive and respectful parenting. She formally studied the Educating RIE Approach and taught Parent-Child classes through Waldorf schools before bringing the content to the virtual platform.

Danielle holds advanced degrees in Early Childhood Development, Holistic Education, Holistic Nutrition, Contemplative Psychology, and has worked in the field with children and families for nearly two decades.

Danielle has touched the lives of numerous families with young children through her holistic coaching method, as well as aspiring mother entrepreneurs. Danielle is a wife, mother, daughter, sister, coach, educator, and friend.

Invitation from the Author

Join a community of like-minded mothers on a mission to serve and grow inside the Patient Connected Mama's Facebook Group to receive ongoing resources, insights, and guidance:

www.facebook.com/groups/patientconnectedmamas

Business Name: The HAP Method

Website: http://www.thehapmethod.com

Facebook URL: www.facebook.com/thehapmethod

Email: danielle@thehapmethod.com

"A great leader must be willing to lead themselves into and through places most others aren't willing to go."

Jenell Lyn Kelly

What if life *is* like a fairytale, a magical story that features fanciful and wondrous characters known as you and me, to teach us valuable lessons? Do you believe you have the power to create the life you desire? Is life but a dream?

I was nine years old as I ran out the wobbly screen door of our big yellow house yelling, "It is going to be the most incredible show ever!" The heat of the summer is brutal in the Northeast, but with adrenaline rushing through my veins I hardly notice it. Heading directly to the left-over plywood from my father's construction jobs, I could picture everything in my mind. The pieces of board were mostly bowed, broken and totally misshapen, but on that day they were perfect. I was going to create a masterpiece with them—a stage for the neighborhood production starring *me*! I could feel the warmth of the sun beating down on my head and the soft green grass squish up between my little toes as I pulled and tugged on the wooden boards, removing them one by one off the uneven stack and dragging them across the backyard. My mind was racing with one creative thought after the other. It didn't matter to me if the boards were uneven, or who was going to play with me or even come to the show. With zero doubt, and not one lick of hesitation, I carried on with my mission—no permission, no one else's opinion was needed—*I trusted my gut, I created my masterpiece, and it was magical!*

If only I was able to continue through life painting into reality the vivid, colorful dreams that ran through my imagination. As the innocence of my childhood years passed, my interactions with the world created an uncertainty in me. The unreciprocated smile or unanswered hello I said to a passerby left me feeling awkward and questioning what was wrong with me. Feelings of being "not enough" started at a young age, leading to self-judgement, self-doubt, and fear. My self-confidence faltered, and at times fear would leave me paralyzed, physically unable to move.

• • •

Years later I'm standing behind the curtain on the big stage of my high school, I can hear the rustling of bodies and the murmurs of voice as the auditorium seats started to fill. My hands are trembling as the heavy red velvet curtain starts to slowly rise and I nervously wait for my cue. As the music plays, I feel frozen in time. Suddenly, and to my complete surprise, a rush of adrenaline runs through my veins and memories of that splendid summer day flash though my mind. I belt out the words to my solo like a songbird in the wind. Freedom, love, and pride fill me as I connect eye to eye with the audience. Applause filled the room as a mighty energy filled the air. It is one of my greatest memories ever!

People had no idea the endless days I spent the year prior in the back of the auditorium in awe of the students who were rehearsing. I was filled with utter amazement, wondering how they could be up there acting and singing in front of others, seemingly without a care in the world. I wanted what they had—that confidence, that uninhibited sense of self and freedom. *My burning desire to experience that level of certainty became greater than my fear!*

• • •

Life goes on, and I can't help but notice the tugging inside of me, the yearning for more than what currently is—and with these desires seem to come great challenges. My social anxiety still creeps in. I think it has become part of who I am, or at least I sometimes allow it to run my life. While all my close friends are getting ready to leave for college, the very thought of it causes me nausea and panic. Lost between teenage years and adulthood, going to college or getting a job, I eventually settled on technical school, and a nursing program of all things! If my younger self were privy to this, she'd be shocked. After all, nursing was the one thing I said I would never do! But it felt like a safe, simple choice, being with the same thirty-six students in the same classroom, on the same schedule.

Who was I kidding? It didn't take long after graduation when a little voice inside started calling out for more. It started as a whisper but grew louder and louder until I could no longer silence it. I was restless and ready to explore!

With my best friend and her future husband in tow, we set off in a U-Haul truck with every belonging I owned jammed inside. This was it; this was the day! No set plans, just a dream and a desire for more. Filled with eagerness, excitement, and a ton of medication as I tried to fight off the flu, we hit the road.

• • •

New adventures led to new love and everything was going well, right up until the day my entire world crashed down around me. I was lying on the floor surrounded by at least a million snotty tissues, feeling like my heart had been ripped out of my chest via my stomach. What was happening? Where did things go wrong? I felt as if an innocence had been taken away. Devasted, sleepless, and feeling like I could barely breathe, I was left to figure out where I was going to live, where I was going to work, even who was I going to hang out with. We had created a life together and we were connected in so many ways.

A few months and a hundred boxes of tissues later, I was finally able to think clearly. I decided to become a travel nurse. The thought of college quickly brings back the familiar feelings of self-doubt. When I say I was clueless to the process of college enrollment, I mean *clueless* with a capital C! I pulled into the overcrowded parking lot of the college with clammy palms and my stomach in knots—just having to find a parking space makes me want to turn around and call it quits. But then I remember why I was there—the empty house, the hurt, the pain that is still resolving, and I am not willing to spend any more time in the past. *I trust if God had me go through it there must be a reason for it.*

Through California, Texas, northern Florida, and all the stops in between, I entered new cities, met new people and learned about so many different nursing techniques, processes, and equipment. It was enough to make me want to cry sometimes, but it also gave me the most incredible set of experiences.

It took a great deal of convincing to get me to take a full-time position back home in southern Florida. I said I would never be in management because it's not why I became a nurse, but Cathy was relentless. As a new ER director she needed an assistant and she wanted me. Seriously, they created a new Assistant Director position just for me! How could I continue saying no?

I was only four months into this new position, I hadn't been lifting anything heavy and wasn't even doing patient care, I can't imagine what I did, but there was a gnawing pain deep inside my left gluteal muscle that was beyond excruciating. I was begging for someone to take their elbow and grind into it to make it go away. The nausea that accompanied it was getting worse. An upcoming holiday meant a welcome four-day weekend, and I was dreaming of being home in a hot bath to soothe the pain. It was around six o'clock on a Friday evening and my legs felt as if they were on fire. I can't seem to change positions to find comfort. I get up to go to the bathroom and the next thing I felt was the carpet under my face. How did I fall? What was happening to me?

The doctor sat me down as we looked at the MRI of my spine. His voice was calm and steady as he pointed at the little gray shadows and explained, "There are fragments of bone scattered everywhere. It will take approximately six weeks to allow the swelling and inflammation to go down before we can go in and try to surgically repair it." My mind swarmed with confusion trying to understand everything but all I can think about is the unbearable pain. How on earth am I going to get through the next six weeks?

My recovery was a battle. The disability company was telling me I no longer had benefits. My medical doctors shrugged their shoulders when I asked questions. I told them I woke up every night in spasms, but they simply dismissed it and offered me another prescription on top of the ones I already refused to fill. How would I know what my body was doing if all I did was mask my symptoms with drugs? I seemed to be the only one concerned.

My insurance called, but I couldn't comprehend the words coming from the soft voice on the other end of the phone. "We have reviewed your records and unfortunately we will no longer be paying for your physical therapy. You just aren't making enough progress. We will be giving you a certificate of disability. Have you considered options other than returning to nursing? Perhaps you can find something that will accommodate your injuries and disabilities." I could feel my heart skip a beat as every cell in my body paused. This time it wasn't fear that paralyzed me but absolute disbelief. WTF? Was this woman insane? The soft voice on the other end of the phone asked, "What are you thinking?" I could barely mumble the words through the rage that was boiling up inside of me. "Who are they?" I asked in a stern yet quiet tone. "Who are they to proclaim my future with limitations, labeling me disabled? Have they met or taken time to speak with me?"

With my home in foreclosure, no income, and my savings going towards recovery, I somehow carried on. *Never once* despite all the pain, the tears, the bout of depression, and the lack of belief from others *did I ever, even for one second, give up on myself.*

I believe our bodies can heal themselves, but it is our minds that often prevent them from doing so.

• • •

I went back to working full time in nursing management. One day as I stood in my office physically, emotionally, and spiritually exhausted, I felt unappreciated and was no longer fulfilled. The inner whisper was calling me once again, but this time it was loud and clear: "I don't want to do this anymore." Every cell in my body rings with agreement. The problem, however, was after twenty-six years in the nursing field I had no idea what else I could do. It wasn't the people I worked with or the hospital I worked for; it was a much deeper calling. My purpose there was done, and it had served me well.

It was December 2017, and I was still wearing nursing scrubs and trusting something was going to change. It took every ounce of my soul to not quit some days. Turning to food to fill emotional voids had been my staple since childhood, and this time wasn't any different. My weight was at an all-time high and my confidence was at an all-time low. I often canceled plans because the stress and the disgust I felt with myself as I stood in my closet trying on one outfit after another, each one either too tight or ill-fitting, brings me to tears and leaves me frustrated. Feelings of "not enough" take over my thoughts.

I ask one of my co-workers, "Okay, what is the stuff you have been telling me about, the supplements, the nutrition, and how do I get it?" I was living paycheck to paycheck with debts up to my ears. I had no desire to learn product details, I was just praying it would work and that I would follow it! The pain of staying where I was far outweighed my resistance to try something new. Isn't that how it is in life? *Only when the pain of staying where we are becomes greater than the payoffs (comforts) we get by staying there does true commitment to change take place.*

January 23, 2017: What in the world was in this stuff? I called Kayla, thanking her for her support and exclaiming how I hadn't felt this good in years! Our conversation took a different turn and she asked me questions about my life, my career, my goals, my passion. It felt a little awkward as no one had ever asked me these types of questions.

Feeling skeptical, judgmental, fearful, and hesitant, but also feeling better than I had in years, I went all-in. I entered the field of network marketing with a company in the health and wellness arena. Sometimes we find what we are looking for, and sometimes it finds us!

I found myself in a community that was larger than life, filled with like-minded, driven, passionate leaders lifting me up every step of the way and allowing me to borrow their unshakable belief as mine continued to grow. As my skepticism passed, my belief in myself grew and I knew I had been given a gift, a kind of "thank you" for all my years of hard work.

Anyone involved in network marketing knows it is essentially self-development with a compensation plan attached—and getting into it is one of the greatest decisions I ever made. Through a beloved member of my team, I was introduced to another mind-blowing community. After completing a three-part course in self-transformation and leadership development, my life completely shifted. The knowing, power, and awareness the trainings instilled in me can hardly be put into words. I am forever grateful for the family, friends, and mentors who entered my life through that community and have lifted me to places I never knew were possible.

• • •

Now it's 2020 and what a journey it has been! It is my first visit to Slide Rock Park in Arizona. Sitting on the warm rocks with my feet in the briskly cold, clear water, I was surrounded by people young and old, all smiling, laughing, some jumping straight off the rocks into the crisp water while others dip their toes in and quickly pull them out. There is something magical about Sedona and it holds a special place in my heart. It's different here as I breathe in the fresh air and bask in the energetic fields of the vortex. The journey to get here has been the most profound experience ever.

I now realize life is one beautiful, blessed journey with every challenge, every experience, the laughter, the tears, the loneliness, and the triumphs. The healing, self-love, and self-nurturing have created growth and expansion greater than I could have imagined. Little did I know that being open to just one opportunity would lead down the path I was longing for. For me, network marketing is a catalyst to self-belief that encourages me to push past every comfort zone I create, and to reach out for others to do the same. My role as a certified transformational trainer is being a guide for others to have and create what they say they want. I am simply a conduit that creates a safe space for people to heal, step into their power, and change the lens through which they view the world.

Our hero's journey begins with an "ah-ha" moment, a bright idea, a yearning for change. Perhaps it's improved health, a relationship, a new business, and so on. Understanding the course of the journey allows for ease, trust, and certainty. But often people hit the brick wall of frustration and give up because they don't realize it is a natural and expected part of the process. Having a well of resources and knowing when to dive deep into them leads down the pathway of achievement! Having brilliant, powerful mentors of my own, in addition to self-resilience, life experiences, and program certifications, are what allow me to provide women the tools to find their voice, claim their power, and achieve what they say they want.

• • •

One simply cannot serve from an empty cup or make withdrawals from an empty bank account. I believe women deserve to look and feel their absolute best and live lives of physical and financial security. As women we tend to constantly place the wants of others ahead of our own, and often we feel the need to "do it all." Our "I got this" mentality leaves us drained and exhausted.

Achieving a healthy mind, body, and bank account starts by fueling your body with proper nutrition and fueling our minds with positive thoughts. Once you discover your passion and follow your calling, your healthy bank account will follow.

There are research-based, proven actions women can use daily to decrease stress, gain more energy, sleep better, reignite their passion, gain increased clarity, and improve their overall wellness.

ABOUT THE AUTHOR

JENELL LYN KELLY

In her thirty-year nursing career Jenell Lyn Kelly empowered her clients through compassion, love, and knowledge. In her four years as an Empowerment Coach and Transformation Trainer, she inspires and empowers not only her medical clients but also fellow nurses and conscious women by providing them the tools and vehicles to improve their physical health, gain clarity, re-ignite their passion, and discover their purpose, leading to the manifestation of new opportunities. Jenell has shared her life changing healthy mind and body principles and practices with fellow nurses and women around the globe.

The proven forty-year-old methodology she incorporates into her coaching and training has been praised for its contribution to the empowerment of women in both their personal and professional lives. Through her participation in The Conscious Influencer's Academy, and as a lead female trainer, Jenell has mentored and coached other powerful women to create fulfilling, impactful, and successful careers as business owners and catalyst coaches.

In addition to supporting and building the transformation community though her volunteer work, Jenell is also a wildly passionate entrepreneur in the field of network marketing. In 2017 she linked arms with one of the most innovative companies in the area of nutrition and healthy lifestyle, which was the turning point in her personal and professional life. Jenell now shares her gifts and pours value into others, supporting them on their journey in the network marketing industry.

Jenell's passion is empowering others to fill their own cup first in order to show up as the best version of themselves for their loved ones, as well as empowering them to share their unique gifts to leave their personal footprint in the world.

Invitation from the Author

Book a complimentary 30-minute Clarity Session with me to start living with optimum health!

https://calendly.com/jenelllyn/30-min

Business Name: Jenell Lyn Enterprises

Website: JenellLyn.com

Facebook URL: https://facebook.com/jenell.kelly.505

Email: JL@jenelllyn.com

"Your success is inevitable. You've already accomplished it. It just needs to unfold now. Allow it to happen. It is time for you to step into your light. You are inevitable."

Hala El Khoury

I look down at a pregnancy test, my heart thumping in my ears. The walls of the public toilet cubicle are very close, and they feel like they're drawing in…closer and closer…I feel a rush of heat rise to my cheeks and my fingertips.

A *very* faint line begins to appear. So faint it's almost invisible. There's no way this is real. I'm twenty. I've been told my whole life to wait.

I've been told my whole life that having children early is a terrible mistake. I feel like my emotions and senses are coated in cotton wool, numbing and muting every sensation. I feel like I'm not allowed to celebrate this pregnancy. It goes against everything that I've been told. I immediately start doing a frantic search online for clinics—abortion clinics.

What about my university degree? I'm so close to finishing! What happens after that? Justin is just starting his five-year degree at university. How are we going to support ourselves? Where would we even live?

I don't even ask Justin what he wants…not right away. I just automatically assumed I have no right to have this baby.

"What do *you* think we should do, Justin?"

"It's your body, I just trust whatever decision you need to make for yourself. But I'm with you no matter what." This is what he is saying out loud, but I can hear in his voice that he too would love to have this baby.

All these overwhelming thoughts are swirling in my head. Spinning, rolling, clouding my mind like a looming storm.

I need to stop and breathe and sit with myself for a moment.

I lie down on my back, taking deep breaths, eyes closed. Suddenly I have a flashback and remember a moment from my childhood. Me at the age of eleven trying to fall asleep:

The warm palms of my hands are resting on my belly while I lay flat on my back. With every deep breath I can feel the rise and fall of my belly. I'm imagining there is a beautiful little baby, growing inside of me with every breath. I am nurturing that baby and breathing life into it.

This is what would calm me down at night when I couldn't sleep.

I realize in that moment, as a multitude of tears stream down my face, that I've always longed for a baby. I've always wanted to be a mom and a nurturer.

After I first shared my longing to have a baby from a young age, I was immediately discouraged by others. And it was mostly other parents—especially my own parents.

"No…it's too soon for you to be thinking about babies. Wait as long as you possibly can. It's not something for you right now. You need to focus on your studies, on your career."

I knew what they meant. I understood it on an intellectual level, sure. But it didn't sit right with me. Some would call it stubbornness. I just felt more determined—a deep knowing in my bones that I can do life—and do it my way.

My parents, out of frustration, would make jokes about me actively *looking* for challenges and looking for the *hard way* to do life.

I *know* that Justin is the one. I've always wanted him as my life partner from the beginning. I know we are destined to do amazing things together, have children together. I can also feel deeply within myself that I am destined to do so much, achieve so much, but not in the conventional way. I've always felt like I was going to do life in a different way.

In this moment I *choose* to stand in my power and do what I want, not what others think I should do.

"I'm moving in with Justin, and that's that. And we're having this baby!"

"Ok…you do you. This is a defining moment for you," my parents responded, no argument, just total acceptance. Wow. That was easy. Maybe that's all I needed—decisiveness.

• • •

I look down and a vivid crimson color captures my attention. That isn't supposed to be there. I know my mom bled when she was pregnant with me, but I was born healthy.

Something feels different here. Something isn't right. The cramps are intense, squeezing and churning. I try to straighten up, but I can't. The stabbing pains are forcing me to hunch over, rounding my back with agony.

"Justin?" I call out to him.

"Yes, baby?" Justin replies from the other room.

"Look…blood" I hear his weight shift as he slides off the chair. The floorboards creak as he comes closer to the bathroom. He looks down, wide-eyed and silent. He takes me into his arms silently and kisses my forehead as I sob and bleed heavily. I try to stop my body from pushing…but the little baby I was growing…with one strong contraction… she's gone.

The vision of a little baby in my arms was fading away…into blackness.

• • •

I wake up, immediately jumping out of bed, something has jolted me to a state of alertness. I feel inclined to pull out a pregnancy test. I'm surprised this is on my mind. We haven't been trying to have a baby.

I look down at the two lines that are forming…and this time, I feel a sense of wholeness. I am ready.

"I met our daughter in my dreams last night…and this pregnancy test says I'm pregnant!"

"What is her name?" Justin's words come out so calmly and naturally.

I pause for a moment. We haven't been thinking about names…I close my eyes. A vision of white block letters over a black background comes to me.

A L M A. "Her name is Alma!"

This time, the news of pregnancy feels like something for which I'm a lot more ready. I saw her in my dreams that night, as if she were telling me, "I'm right here."

• • •

"I really wish you had waited. You're right in the middle of your PhD and your diploma of counselling." Those words fall on my ears and settle there for a moment. I'm not sure what to say.

The baby is here. It's not like I can reverse being pregnant just because people I love think the timing is a "mistake."

I feel a sizzling of anger—or maybe disappointment—because I know deep down inside that being pregnant doesn't mean my studies or my career will take a hit. I don't believe it.

Why can't people just be happy for me, and leave it at that?

I've always wondered why people feel they need to give their unwanted opinions, especially to pregnant women.

But the days are flowing from one to the next. I finished getting my qualification as a counsellor. My PhD has been coming along very well. I'm working on a brand-new area of expertise—my supervisor and I are pioneers in the field of neuroregeneration. Looking back, I know I always wanted to study something unique, something scientific but also empowering.

And I've been teaching at the university too. I love teaching neuroanatomy. I love it when the eyes of my students light up when I talk them through the structures in the brain, show it to them, and then quiz them. It's so satisfying. The pay is great, too.

But something is constantly lingering in my mind. This isn't a job I can keep up. I look down at my growing belly that bears Alma. All I can do at this time is just keep hustling. Keep teaching. Keep making good money as a nest egg—savings to fall back on when work is no longer a possibility.

• • •

Justin steps into our room while I nurse a three-week-old Alma, "Hala, I have a call booked for us, can you make yourself available for 2:00 pm?"

"Uh…sure…but what is this about?" I can hear some suspicion in my voice.

"It's about high ticket closing and entrepreneurship."

"Is this another program you want us to pay for? You know I don't like investing in random things I know nothing about! We already have a whole bunch of programs we haven't even used." My tone is now frustrated.

"This one is different…just promise me you'll keep an open mind."

I'm on the call with Justin, Alma in my arms, and I don't know why this is happening, but I feel a sense of determination—the same type of determination that fueled me all these years.

All this time, the concept of entrepreneurship and doing life on my own terms has been brewing quietly in the corner. And now, being on this call with a "closer" (not a typical salesperson), I can feel all my beliefs in myself being pulled to the surface.

Justin is looking over at me with his smiling eyes and open smile, teeth showing, trying to understand where my mind is right now. He looks excited. I love that smile he makes. It's so Justin.

"Okay."

"What was that?" replies the closer on the phone and Justin's eyes and smile widen.

"I said okay. Let's do it. I need to move forward and grow. And I can't go back to university anytime soon."

This is it. I'm going to learn a new, scalable skill that will empower me to work from home. My own hours.

The feeling of peaceful excitement washes over me. I feel a deep sense of knowing I'm going to take this and make the most of it. I must.

• • •

I'm trained as a High Ticket Closer. I stumble across this incredible influencer, Danielle Leslie. I love her style, her energy, and the kind of community she attracts and keep her in mind right from the beginning of my journey. I feel within myself that one day I may close for her and work with her.

The moment I finished my training, I'm immediately head-hunted by another woman who has a coaching program that helps people transition into better-paying jobs as business analysts. She asks me to close for her coaching program.

Wow—that was quick! But the feeling of excitement and accomplishment was beginning to be replaced with dread. I started taking calls and found out the leads weren't well-informed or prepared. I wasn't having a good time with this account. It turns out people were misinformed, and I felt so alone taking these calls. I wasn't in my area of passion. And now I'm so overwhelmed because things have started to feel toxic for me. I'm not enjoying myself.

Alma is four months old and she can sense my attention isn't all on her. I can feel her frustration.

One day, I was in the middle of taking back-to-back calls. I step away for one second and suddenly hear a "thud" as Alma hits the ground—she's fallen about thirty centimeters onto the wooden floorboards! A split second of silence and then her cries erupt as if to say, "You weren't watching me! You let that happen to me! I am so hurt right now. How could you let that happen?"

Mid-sentence with the woman on the phone, I instinctively leap to my feet and run over to Alma to snatch her tiny little body into my arms, cradling her. As she wails, I immediately tell the client on the phone that I'll have to get back to her. I think she was relieved to be getting off the phone, to be honest.

Left to myself and Alma's cries, I sob with her, sinking low onto the bed, feeling like the worst mom in the world.

I thought this type of career would give me more freedom, and instead I'm spending countless hours on the phone with people who weren't qualified for a program that isn't my passion. I'm letting myself down. I'm letting the coach down. I'm letting Justin down. And more than anyone else, I feel I'm letting Alma down.

Despite making some sales and generating some income, I'd be constantly waking up with dread. I'd be sacrificing my attention towards Alma.

I am not doing what I love. I don't love talking to people who think they are going to get a quick fix. I don't love doing these calls for free, only earning on a commission basis, giving so much of my heart and time without it being truly valued—and I am *letting* it happen.

A couple of months pass by and that account falls through. I loved the coach, but we weren't benefiting from each other anymore and it just wasn't an ideal fit.

I realized in that moment I needed to be working for *myself*, for something I *love*, something within my scope.

I have something to offer. Mindset. Empowerment. Personal growth.

At this point of realization, I begin posting on social media. I begin posting on LinkedIn. Videos of myself speaking my mind and adding value, spreading words of encouragement that I *know* people need to hear, because I needed to hear it too. Within the three months, my following organically grew from 100 to 10,000 followers. They like my content. They're engaging with it. People are starting to recognize me out in public from my videos on LinkedIn!

But here's the problem. I get fifty-plus messages in my inbox per day, two hundred connection requests per day—all this interest but no product to give them! What is even my offer?

People on LinkedIn started expecting me to post on a regular basis. I'd also be receiving flirtatious messages in my inbox, just for being a visible female.

Once again, I'm finding myself dedicating a lot of time without getting anything in return. It's not coming from my heart anymore, but as a sense of obligation, because people are expecting to be entertained by my videos.

I start to feel burnt out and exhausted. But I'm feeling *very* unusually exhausted.

And then *another* positive pregnancy test enters my life.

Ah...*that's* why I'm so exhausted and nauseous!

To top things off, then COVID-19 hits. Justin and I move houses right in the midst of it. We moved out of his parents' home where we had the comfort of not paying rent to our own space where we needed to keep ourselves accountable by paying rent.

Suddenly, I see a rise in work from home opportunities. Since I'm not making much money at all for my family, I start looking at online job listings. Positions that offer thirty-five dollars per hour on casual contract. Job interviews. But something constantly doesn't feel right. I'm selling myself short.

I need it for the consistency. But every time I look at another job offer and the requirements, I see all the sacrifices of my time I need to make. Every time, my heart just sinks. It doesn't feel right.

I need to be working for myself—towards something that's going to *build* me, towards something that's going to *help* my family, towards something that suits me.

I wake up one morning, recently after moving, and open my phone. There's an email from Danielle Leslie. I've been following her for a year now. "I'm hiring" was the subject line. WHAT?!

I jump out of bed, ruffle my curls, and make a job application video, being my authentic speaker self, putting to good use all the communication skills I've learnt from posting my videos daily on LinkedIn.

• • •

I am selected for the next round, and then the next round, and then I get an email saying that I've been selected to be a part of the closing team. A *team*. That's what I've been wanting for so long now—an environment where I can learn from amazing people like Danielle, speak to amazing clients who *know* who they're following and want the product.

Excitement!

And results. I am getting results. I'm closing clients into the biggest investments they've ever made in their lives!

There would be days where I feel like a *total failure*!

And there would be days where I would feel incredible and inspirational, days where I would get on the phone with a client I thought would never commit or move forward, but when she spoke to me, she *did it*. She was inspired, emotional, motivated, and excited because she felt heard and I helped bring to the surface what was sitting deep within her—a knowing that she's destined for more.

I always knew that I wanted to coach people, but I never knew where to begin. This was a direct window. By closing for Danielle, I was learning. I've been feeling so happy, challenged every day. The launch was a success! I earned a lot of money, but I also realized I actually knew how to coach people to get out of their own way and *get results*.

• • •

Whether you already have kids, or you have been told to wait to have kids, this is my message for you:

You are strong.

You are capable.

And there's something deep inside of you that already knows you are destined for more.

It is a challenging journey, and a lot of people get stuck along the way, thinking they've failed.

You have not failed.

In fact, you are so close! All you need are five things:

1. The deep why: This is the purpose behind what you want to do.
2. Self-worth and a healthy relationship with money.
3. A marriage between the first two to identify what your unstoppable strategy is and what you offer.
4. To know how to attract the right people who love your essence, need your services and then knowing how to get them as your clients.
5. A supportive environment that supports you, honors you, and keeps you accountable.

I decided to put to use all the things I've learnt. All the heartache, the challenges, and make them accessible to other women because this is what I wished I had when I was starting out.

You've probably felt that there's more you are destined for; it can be intimidating when entering this world…but we are so much stronger when we support each other!

ABOUT THE AUTHOR

HALA EL KHOURY

Hala El Khoury is a business coach for women who are coaches or destined to be coaches. Her approach is to help these women fearlessly step into their authentic power and potential.

With her three-week-old firstborn daughter nursing in her arms, she attained High Ticket Closing qualifications from Dan Lok, trained under Kerwin Rae's business program, and collaborated with fellow coaches to help them level up their businesses and share their essence more deeply.

Hala originally started in a traditional academic background with a Bachelor of Medical Science, majoring in Immunology and Neuroscience. She taught neuroanatomy at the University of Sydney, and her PhD was in the field of neuroscience, in particular neuroregeneration. Hala also has a diploma in Counselling, specializing in expressive therapy, parenting, and couples counselling.

Although academia was always a major part of her earlier years, starting a family at the age of twenty-three inspired her to enter the world of online coaching and influencership. She uses her background to create a deeply nurturing, holistic and transformative experience with her clients.

Being a woman, a wife, and a mother who didn't want to sacrifice her time or her self-worth, Hala plunged into her new career of coaching. It is her mission to guide women (especially those having or planning to have children) to confidently step into their fearless authenticity despite the sacrifices society expects of them.

Invitation from the Author

Get in touch to start a conversation. I want to be there for you!

I also want to offer you my free eBook to help you with your journey:

https://halaelkhoury.myportfolio.com/contact

Business Name: Hala El Khoury - Fearlessly Authentic Coaching

Website: https://halaelkhoury.myportfolio.com/

Facebook URL: https://www.facebook.com/Auralala

Email: elkhouh.13@gmail.com

"Get out of your OWN way."

Kristin Sullivan

I inherited my Grandmothers gift of intuition—the ability to pay very close attention to those feelings that hit you like a brick dropping in your gut, the warm itchy sweat beading up in the palms of your hands, or the solid lump forming in your throat that almost takes your breath away. It's that feeling you get when you just know from your own senses that something is off and trying to push you out of your comfort zone, or what I now understand as a shift in my alignment. I contribute much of my success as a wedding planner to that very same gift. It is a gift that has always allowed me time to prepare, to switch gears into what I refer to as "survival mode" or plan B! I am personally a dog lover, and yet very much like a cat, I always land on my feet. I have lived nine lives before the age of forty-nine, but don't worry, this will be the short version of my story!

I left high school in the eleventh grade because I thought I was bored. I have learned since then that I most likely had ADD. I could never focus on just one thing and my mind was always racing off in another direction (or three). I was street smart with good grades, and I was one of the most popular kids, being friends with others from all walks of life, but I was lost, so I quit. Instead of attending school, I worked two jobs while getting my GED. I remained connected with all of my friends, some of which are still my very best friends today. Years later I even went on to college. It was there I finally found a focus and passion for business, but I quit that too! With just two classes left I was presented with an opportunity to buy a local travel agency. I had always loved to travel, and the agency opportunity had a certification program as well.

It was 1997 when I bought the travel agency and became a certified travel agent and small business owner. I am not sure the certification process even exists as a true license any longer. As luck would have it, just shortly after the agency purchase, the travel industry was dealt a swift kick in the ass by the airlines when travel bookings shifted online after the internet emerged. This giant shift forced most smaller shops to eventually close their doors. It was survival time, and I had just invested all I had to get deeply involved in my local community. At the time, I was the youngest person ever to sit on the Board of Directors for the local Chamber of Commerce, and I was one of the only ladies in the local Rotary chapter. I won Female Young Careerist and had big plans. Needless to say, I had to think fast and figure out a solution to keep business alive.

It was then that I decided to turn my passion for gatherings and celebrations into a boutique agency specializing in groups. During this same time, I was personally struggling with my relationship. I was dating a man nineteen years older than me who was a very successful business owner. Our age gap and where we were at in business didn't align. We struggled for many years and thought getting married would fix things. In January of 2001 we wed on Little Palm Island in the Florida Keys, and it was a nightmare! This resurfaced later in my nine lives and is the key reason why I became a wedding planner.

The agency downturn continued to be a big stress point in my marriage with the industry taking such a blow. Even though I had married a man of great wealth, I took a full-time position as Global Travel and Events Manager for another local based business and enjoyed traveling worldwide. I was in this position on September 11, 2001. We were headquartered in New Hampshire, with offices outside of Boston, which meant our travelers used Boston and Portland airports on a daily basis. It is a day I, like most, will never forget. I slept on my office floor that night as we manually went through our previous months of paper computer printouts to track each possible traveler. Our travel reservation system was American Express and had gone down, which meant we had no way to easily track our travelers.

It was a very frightening time for all, I was asked to fly within a week to attempt to curb fear of traveling in support of the company culture. I recall vomiting in the airport bathroom that morning and boarding a nearly empty flight where I sat in complete silence from Boston to Little Rock and back. I left that position shortly afterwards and expanded my own travel agency to include destination management services inbound to New England. In 2004 my husband and I divorced, and I sold the agency and moved to Key West. The years I spent in the Keys would make for a series of books on their own—from divorce to business failings, business partnerships falling apart, a second marriage, and second divorce—that series offers more drama than a soap opera!

In addition to destination weddings, I began traveling for destination sporting events and overseeing luxury events in the automotive space while living bi-coastal for a few years between San Diego and Key West to escape the madness (we called it "getting off the rock"). When I finally landed back in Florida full-time after several roller coaster relationships, I met someone I thought was "the one." He was in law enforcement and appeared safe and honest, unlike the last few.

On the outside, we looked like we were living a fairytale life. We resided full time on a private island with no rent or mortgage, no utility costs, and no maintenance costs. We took a boat to and from work each day, allowing us to catch both the sunrise and the sunset. We shared a private beach and a dock (he had two of his own boats), we traveled, and we had recently paid cash for a waterfront lot in the Bahamas where we planned to build a second home. While the home was being designed, we were awaiting the conclusion of a long, painful, drawn-out international legal and permitting process. Thankfully, this delay also caused a delay in the beginning of any construction. While on a fishing trip in the Florida Keys with friends, we got news we were unable to secure the funding for the build—turns out it is very difficult to get lending for property located outside of the U.S. We had just finalized the home design plans and had cleared the lot. I thought I could figure out a way to make it all come together but exhausted all options.

Ultimately, he held this against me, and it turned into anger and nonsupport of what I wanted to do in business. He was resentful, distant, and shut down. For months I suspected he was having an affair with someone he worked with, which was later confirmed. When I look back now, I realize this was both another intuitive sign and a blessing in disguise. One month later Hurricane Dorian, the strongest hurricane to ever make landfall, sat stalled over the Bahamas for hours upon hours and destroyed the island. Many lives were lost, many dreams were shattered and washed away during that deadly storm. The land was put up for sale and would be the only reason for us to ever communicate with each other going forward.

I sank into a pretty dark space after things ended between us. This was the fifth time in my life I had run from a committed relationship to include two engagements and two marriages. Today I know this stems from the deeper trauma in my life of having never met my biological father. I know who he is and even reached out a few years back. I attempted to connect but he never followed through. He never married my mother as they were too young. He was married to another woman and, ironically, they gave their daughter almost the same first name as me. I considered my maternal grandfather to be my real father. Later in life I learned he had also been unfaithful to my grandmother, which devastated me. My mother married a man who adopted me when I was young, but he also had an affair and then turned into a dead-beat dad who never paid child support and had other children and additional marriages. You can follow how there is a hurtful pattern here with men in my life. I have been in and out of therapy for years. I did think the last one was going to work, but he had even more baggage than I did with his three failed marriages. I know we cross paths with people for a reason in life, and hopefully someday I will know what this path taught me. After we broke up, I learned he had a child he never told me about. Just when you think you know someone, you really don't!

With all that said, I picked myself up, dusted myself off and thought I had finally figured it all out. Things were turning around and seemed to be falling perfectly into place for 2020, I am a big fan of double digits. I found a home on the water that fit my master plan. I knew it needed a bit of love, but I was just excited to have a place of my own with the ability to build out an Airbnb unit and set my business plans into motion. I closed on the house, hired a contractor to gut the downstairs space, and bought a vintage camper to set up as my onsite mobile office. It even matched my business vison-branding board! I had set a deadline to be up and running by April 1st and wanted it to be a well-oiled machine prior to my departure for my destination retreats launching in June. Gutting the house revealed a bit more than expected, which should really be expected in any renovation project, but I kept forging ahead while watching my savings account dwindle down.

As someone who has traveled most of her career, I knew what was important as a guest. I spent months staying in Airbnb's, researching and documenting in preparation for this. It was finally time to get it listed and start paying down that mortgage, which was part of my overall business plan. I had finished the package details for what I named "planning-moons," which are wedding planning retreats for couples. I had scheduled a photo shoot. The staging and decorating were perfectly done down to every last detail. I was so proud of the design and reuse of space. It made me happy to go sit down there and envision brides and grooms escaping to come sit and relax on their private deck overlooking the water, watching for manatees, dolphins, turtles, and the occasional alligator. They would end their day with a view of the sky on fire above, witnessing breathtaking sunset views after a day of planning their wedding in a calm and stress-free setting.

I am not one to watch the news each morning as I feel like it just starts my day off hearing only the bad things happening around the world. Afterall, I had made it my mission in 2020 to start each day with a positive routine of meditation, yoga, journaling, drinking Rev (a clean energy drink), taking my Usana supplements, and diving into my online advanced business education program. I turned the computer on, logged in, and felt one of those strange feelings come over me, something was not right. I began to scan social media and for the first time read the word "coronavirus." To be honest, I recall sitting there and saying to myself, "Well, I don't recall the last time I drank a Corona (the beer) so I should be just fine." Then for a fleeting moment I checked my stock account as I had purchased Anheuser-Busch stock and recalled reading they owned the Corona production company. Needless to say, things were not looking good.

As I learned more about what was happening, my survival instinct once again started to kick in. I turned my focus to all the weddings and events over the next thirty days and what I would do to protect that client experience. What I could never have imagined at that time was looking over the next 300 days and how my master plan for everything was about to implode. No opening of the Airbnb, no planning-moons, no traveling for retreats, no new wedding planning clients, just refunds, cancellations, and a lack of sleep wondering how this could be happening!

I fell off the morning health routine fast and instead planted myself in front of the television in my pajamas all hours of the day watching the world collapse around me. I listened to a business analyst talk about filing for a mortgage forbearance and did so immediately. I did the same with my mobile office and my vehicle. I applied for the payroll protection program (PPP) and waited. As a small business owner, we are the ones who got hit the hardest. We all fell between the government cracks of zero help for main street. I was denied—denied while other companies received, in some cases, multiple loans with fraudulent documentation.

You know how they say bad news comes in threes? Well, the same week the denial happened would kick off the rainy season in Florida, and that is when the shit really started to hit the fan. My brand new beautiful little rental unit began to leak. The perfect white beadboard ceiling was ruined. The rain kept coming and the leaks appeared in multiple places throughout the house. I shed a tear for every raindrop that dripped into my home. I thought I had done everything right. I had every inspection done before buying the house. I relied on the professionals to do what they do. Sadly, I ended up with a lemon—a lemon of a house, a lemon of an inspection company, and ultimately a lemon of a contractor. But wait, there's more! Over the course of the next couple of weeks I wandered around the lemon house in a constant state of shock. The repairs I needed to do were more than fifty thousand dollars! My savings were gone after the down payment, the move, and the original renovation project. I had maxed out both credit cards (equaling another fifty thousand dollars) and I started to panic.

But then I remembered who I was, and my survival mode kicked in. I am a *planner*, and I needed a damn plan! I started to think about what I would do if I couldn't rent my unit or hold my weddings and retreats. I briefly thought about pivoting (a word I now detest more than the word Corona) to a virtual retreat, but just the thought of sitting in front of a camera for hours at a time gave me instant anxiety, I am a behind-the-scenes girl for a reason. I tossed that idea right out the window.

I read story after story of colleagues and mentors shutting down their physical offices, selling their homes, and some even closing their doors for good. By nature as planners, we just do not sit still well—we are constantly thinking and juggling for others. In my case, I know it is a coping mechanism from childhood—a way to take the focus off looking at myself and my own journey. Having that taken away from me forced onto another path inward, which scared the hell out of me. I tried hard to stay focused on something by keeping up with my online business schooling. I honestly do believe this (along with my puppy Abaco) saved my life, and I will forever be grateful and thankful for my business coach, Lisa Johnson. I needed real-life, zero-bullshit guidance from someone who had weathered storm after storm and survived. Lisa gave me the inspiration, the tools, and the kick in the ass I needed to make a plan.

It was always my intention to launch a retail line once the retreats were up and running. Well, I had plenty of time on my hands now to start using those sleepless nights to do what I do best, which is to plan and create. I started with the 9P11 bag, an event planning emergency kit created for planners to use onsite/on their person while working at events. Being a person for years who searched for dresses with deep pockets to hide the necessities, this was a top mission of mine.

I already carried a kit—an amazing fully stocked kit—but running around with a kit that weighed thirty pounds was a nightmare and stuffing my pockets full of items only resulted in losing things. I have lost keys, cash, credit cards, and so much more. This was the inspiration behind the 9P11 bag—911 for emergency and the P for Planners. This is my high-ticket retail item. It comes fully stocked and ready to go. It is important to note that a portion of the profits from all my products, despite financial situations, will be donated to various charities. The charities selected for the 9P11 are

The Chapel of Honor and The Voices of September 11 organization.

Next in production, after more than two decades as a planner, is my wedding planning guide and journal, simply called "A Wedding Journal – Something Us." For years I witnessed people struggle with where to keep important notes about their wedding details, and I also encourage daily journaling about their wedding plans. I wanted to give people a tool they would use and cherish. A Wedding Journal is something meant to be left out as a coffee table book reflecting a couple's story and wedding planning journey. I personally chose and commissioned the artwork to coincide with a planning timeline. This is my mid-ticket retail item. A portion of the journal profits will go to bringing book fairs to impoverished schools. Book fairs were always my favorite days in school.

Lastly, while needing to fill another few sleepless nights, I decided to take a creative mental break by signing up for a class on how to create your own affirmation card pack. I aimed to provide a solution for those who cannot perhaps afford a wedding planner or simply do not want one. My card packs are a very mini version of my retreat business in a pretty little package. They also represent my low-ticket retail item. These cards advise people on what to do during the final thirty days before their wedding. A portion of the card pack profits will be donated to The Chapel of Honor, a charity I created to gift free weddings to Veterans.

I am still sitting in construction hell, and now in the middle of hurricane season. The Airbnb roof has been "fixed" three different times now but is still not repaired. My contractor has been fired for ghosting and not providing any of the documentation I keep asking for. The painter he hired never finished the job after I asked him twice to make sure he covered my new vintage camper before spraying, and of course I came home to find spray all over it. I had to hire someone on the side to finish enclosing the screened-in deck and install a new door. I have a giant mound of wasted sand from the stucco mix sitting in my driveway melting away each time it rains, which is a daily afternoon occurrence. My dog fence lines were cut when they were digging for the concrete footers and instead of telling me they simply unplugged it! My security system is down to one working camera since they have not rehung anything after the stucco went up. Now mind you this is a guy who came highly recommended! This is a guy who lives just minutes away from here. This is a guy for whom I had lined up two other neighbors' upcoming projects for him and would have given him the renovation of my kitchen and three bathrooms (none of which will happen now). What is wrong with people? I am sitting here in survival mode and these contractors do not ever show up or finish anything. I thought 2019 was bad, but 2020 is coming in hot for first place.

I am only allowing for great things from here on out. For all of you reading this today, I say to you, keep going! Keep pushing yourself past your fears and your comfort zones and do not give up. Fail, get back up, and fail again! Each time I failed I learned something and got up stronger than before. Love yourself first and take care of *you* first. Establish a morning routine and do your very best to never compromise your beliefs or give up on your dreams. And lastly, pay close attention to your intuition—be guided by those gut feelings and awkward moments when your body is resisting—and let it lead you.

ABOUT THE AUTHOR

KRISTIN SULLIVAN

For more than two decades "Chief Celebration Officer" Kristin Sullivan of Swivel Group Events has been executing destination celebrations to remember, designing unforgettable weddings, milestone birthdays, anniversaries, and corporate VIP experiences for thousands of couples and corporate clients. Kristin has expanded into the world of wellness, marrying it to wedding planning by creating The Bridal Retreat. With a heart full of hospitality, she also created an intimate bed and breakfast solely for couples to escape for a "planning-moon." Kristin is the weekly host of Leftovercakechat on YouTube, has been quoted on People.

com, featured in several magazines, and one of her weddings was featured on ABC Primetime. She spent the 2020 pandemic creating and producing her retail line to include a planner emergency tool bag, a set of wedding planning + wellness cards, and a wedding journal. Kristin loves spending time with her dog Abaco and is passionate about traveling.

Invitation from the Author

Visit my website for complimentary planning tools to help you create the celebration of your dreams:

https://www.thebridalretreat.com/connect/

Business Name: The Bridal Retreat

Website: https://www.thebridalretreat.com/

Facebook URL:
https://www.facebook.com/shecomesfromboston

Email: kristin@thebridalretreat.com

"You are worthy. There are no ifs or buts. No matter what has happened in the past. You have always been worthy and deserve a full and happy life. End of story."

Samantha Popp

Did you know you will continue to repeat the same situations until you fully heal from them? The pattern will proceed over and over again until you make a change to stop the cycle. It's 2014 and I see my whole life ahead of me. All the amazing things I can create for myself and so much excitement about what the future holds. I'm working on figuring out what I want to do with my life and who's going to be beside me to help me take on the world.

It's not an easy task to figure out what your purpose is, and if you surround yourself with people who don't want to support you or your purpose, then it adds extra stress to your life. You don't want to struggle in your journey, so you try to get through it with a support system to help you through all wavelengths you experience along the way. A supportive partner is a bonus cherry on top to help you feel unstoppable.

I crave a real man in my life. One who loves and respects me for everything I am, who supports me in everything, and who accepts my body completely. I think I have found it in this guy, Matt. Things are starting off good—he makes me laugh until my stomach hurts. He looks at me with those soft hazel eyes and I feel my knees getting weak. He makes me melt like butter sitting out on a hot summer day in Texas.

A good start—right up until he hits me for the first time. I put on my favorite turquoise blouse that really pops with my skin tone and he sees me. His eyes fill with rage.

"What the fuck are you wearing?" Matt belittles me.

"It's what I'm wearing tonight. Why?" I ask, shrugging my shoulders.

His nostrils flare and I can practically see the steam coming out of his ears. He slaps me so hard across my right cheek I feel it get hot and red immediately. My eyes sting from the tears welling up like a pool and my vision gets blurry. The energy spewing from Matt terrifies me and I stay cowering on the floor while holding the right side of my face in disbelief.

Matt crouches down to my level and I'm trying to scoot myself backwards away from him. He whispers in my ear, "Never provoke me like that again or I'll hit you harder and do some real damage."

I am in complete shock. I have never seen this side of him until now and he makes it seem like it's all my fault, but is it my fault? No. No, it's definitely not. I didn't take his hand and hit myself. HE HIT ME, and that's wrong. That's not how a true man treats his girlfriend. I need out, but how do I leave him? I need to make a plan. I know I can do this.

His new job in Atlanta provides space and distance between us and he hasn't put his hands on me in a while. It brings me a splinter of peace while I'm coming up with my escape plan. I don't even know how many times he's laid his hands on me, but I still know in my soul it's the right thing to leave him. I go through a million different scenarios of how I can leave him and none of them work out. I can't do it in person because it'll fire up the anger in his belly and the only thing I'll gain is more bruises. No. That is not going to happen again. I will not let it. He doesn't deserve me, but he thinks he can take advantage of my kindness. NO WAY.

I find all the courage that has always been inside me from the moment I was born and I pick up the phone to call him and end it. I never, not for one second thought I'm weak or a coward for doing it this way. I'm out! I'm safe! He can't hurt me anymore! That's the end of my abusive relationship. I can find my true soulmate who would never lay a hand on me.

I think it's all over because I'm gone, I left him, and now I find comfort in alcohol. Partying every night and getting hammered with my girlfriends at the hottest bars in the city. I inhale vodka on those nights and dance with stranger after stranger who offer kind whispers to me about how hot I look in my outfit while sliding their hands all over my body. I think this is okay and healthy for me to do for myself. I allow these dirtbags to use my body because I still feel unworthy of love. I accept this behavior from random guys. But then Andrea asks me out for coffee.

We meet up at our favorite local coffee place, The Lazy Loaf, and she indulges me with some small talk. Andrea asks me how my dog is doing, and I ask her how school is going. She looks at me like she has something stuck in her throat and she's trying to find the right words. Her words come out like a bomb, confronting me about my partying problem.

"I hate to see you throw everything away and flush it all down the toilet," Andrea reveals.

I felt like I was just hit by the morning garbage truck. My eyes widen, my heart is pounding, and breathing feels impossible. This is bad. My best friend in the world is calling me out on my shit.

She repeats, "This lifestyle is destroying you and I can't stand to watch you go down this path that will end up killing you."

Andrea reminds me of how dangerous all my choices are. I never really thought what I'm doing is so destructive. I just want to enjoy myself and be in the moment. I'm not thinking of the consequences of my actions until RIGHT NOW. She opened my eyes to the dark path I'm on and the final destination. I don't want my story to end that way and I will not let it end that way.

• • •

It's 2017 and the ground is just starting to thaw. I tell myself I'm over Matt and I'm ready to get into another relationship. I think I'm ready to handle it.

I'm back on the dating wagon looking for my "Mr. Right" in the big ol' sea. There's so many fish out there and one of them has got to be the right guy for me. That's when Zack came along. He's so sweet and always makes time to see me. I think to myself, "How wonderful is this?"

Tonight's our first date and I'm just finishing getting ready. I put on my favorite fitted seafoam dress that accentuates my body in all the right places and shows off my big, strong thighs. He texts me that he's going to be fifteen minutes late. I think it's no big deal until it's an hour-and-a-half later. My stomach is growling and I'm irritated, but the moment I see him pull up and nonchalantly walk to my front door with a bouquet of flowers, all is forgiven—but not forgotten.

I let it slide, along with other little things indicating his disrespect for me until I say the wrong thing and he explodes like a bomb. Screaming at the top of his lungs inches away from my face, I attempt to hold in the tears welling up inside.

I'm crying on average once a week if not more during the really bad weeks. Trying to tiptoe on the eggshells that are his emotions and ego so I can avoid getting screamed at. It's fucking killing me. I'm miserable and he's always so unpredictable. It makes me question how I got here.

I hit my limit and I need out. I finally feel the fire in my belly getting bigger. All the courage I was born with is coming back to me from my core. It's about to explode out of me. I'm so here for it. Last night was the last time he was ever going to yell at me again. I do not accept being treated like this. It's time to create another escape plan, but this one is going to be much different. This time I must move out my stuff, but that's okay. I can do it. I have it in me to leave this abusive relationship like the previous one and nothing is going to stop me.

Today's the day! Zack is gone on a job and I have the place to myself. My friend Andrea is coming to help me move my stuff, so it'll be much faster than by myself. I don't have to do anything alone and I'm so grateful she's helping me with this. She'll be here in an hour so I'm starting to pack up my stuff in whatever containers I can find.

From start to finish my heart felt like it was going to beat out of my chest. My anxiety felt like it was higher than it ever has been before. I'm sweating through my grey V-neck T-shirt, running all over the house gathering up all my things and moving boxes. I remind myself there's enough time to get all the items important to me out of the house. Nothing is going to stop me from leaving. Once I lock the door, I'm NEVER coming back.

The finish line feels so close! Here we go! My body is slowly tiring out from moving all my items with Andrea. After moving the last box out of the car and into my new place, a big weight has been lifted off me—not just physically, but mentally and psychologically. To leave that place and Zack was an incredible feeling. The anxiety of having to walk on eggshells around his ego is gone. All the worry and fear about staying in that house and being abused is melting away.

It's official: I'm long gone now. I think I've won the war, but there's another battle to be won. Zack has been texting and calling my cell at all hours of the day and night, keeping me on my toes constantly. I feel the hairs stand up on the back of my neck wondering if he's going to physically try to find me. He's using all the "right" words and charismatic behaviors to manipulate me to come back to him—attempting to get under my skin and emotions so I come crawling back. At this point he's making my skin crawl and I cringe at the thought of his rough hands touching me anywhere on my body.

Everything good he made me feel is gone. It won't work this time, Zack. I'm not coming back. EVER. All that is left now is the yelling and belittlement you put me through and it's over. I will not let you reel me back into the hell-hole you put me in. I'm done. I don't deserve to ever feel this way again, and I won't. I promise myself I will not let this happen ever again.

He's been harassing me for too damn long. I'm so exhausted from being woken up at 3:00 am and it's time to end this. I pick up my cell and press the numbers on my screen with irritation. He answers. I feel my heart start to beat faster and louder. I'm thinking to myself, "Can I do this? Yes. Yes I can." Suddenly, all the words I have always wanted to say to both Matt and Zack come flowing out of me like a river in the spring right after the ice melts. I'm filled with pride and empowerment for speaking up for myself and sticking to my boundaries.

• • •

It's 2020 and I'm a relationship coach helping other women recognize unhealthy relationships so they can leave and call in the true love of their life. Focusing on myself and making my needs a priority has been the best decision I've ever made. I've made so much progress in just the past couple months. I feel like I can breathe again. I'm letting go of all the trauma and abuse that has ever been imposed upon me and damn it feels good. Better than good, it feels amazing. I am finally becoming this empowered woman I was always created to become. Here she is.

I no longer ask for permission from others. I only ask for permission from myself. I make decisions that are good for me regardless of what others say. I'm embracing my voice and making it known that my voice matters. I found my authenticity, so I don't hide any part of myself anymore. I show up as the amazing woman I've always been. And most importantly, under any and all circumstances, I persevere. I choose to be a woman who can help other women do the same and stop playing small in their own life.

You too can heal from your past and become an empowered woman to call in the love of your life just like I did! Let's do it together so you can give yourself the best chance of achieving the most amazing life. Be the woman who chooses herself every time and never feels ashamed of it.

ABOUT THE AUTHOR

SAMANTHA POPP

Samantha Popp is a Relationship and Sex Coach specializing in helping women re-ignite their inner fire and build confidence so they can experience passion, fulfillment, and THE BEST SEX LIFE ever! She's an international bestselling author of *The Success Rituals: Winning Habits of High-Achieving Women*, a domestic abuse survivor, eating disorder recovery warrior, founder of the women's empowerment community There She Glows, and creator of The Glow Up Method.

She helps women ditch their inner critic, level up their intimate relationships, and live EMPOWERED AF. Samantha believes that making yourself a priority is the first step in creating a wild and wonderful life and relationship.

Invitation from the Author

Visit my FREE Women's Empowerment Community on Facebook to receive resources and insights to empower you:

https://www.facebook.com/groups/2573558742693756

Business Name: Samantha Popp Coaching

Website: https://samanthapopp.podia.com/

Facebook URL: https://www.facebook.com/Samanthapoppcoach/

Email: samanthapoppcoaching@gmail.com

"Never assume another single person possesses the same passion and drive in reaching your destiny. It's all up to you."

Dana Peever

That year will be etched in her memory forever. As the skeletons came tumbling out of the closet, one after the other, she wasn't sure she could handle much more. It left her feeling like a shell of her usual confident, poised self. She thought those feelings of worthlessness were long gone, having been acknowledged and dealt with twenty-five years ago. It wasn't like her to need help. She prided herself on the level of independence she'd forged throughout her lifetime, always being the person others went to for assistance. The tables had turned, and it left her with an uneasy feeling deep in the pit of her stomach.

She got through a good part of that year with the help of her next-door neighbor. Their daily lunchtime walks allowed for dissection of the circumstances surrounding the fall of each skeleton. At one point, they both acknowledged that their conversations might not be enough. Luckily, the neighbor was able to provide the perfect referral.

Her new therapist provided the reset she needed to forge ahead. Armed with tools and homework, she left her first session feeling more encouraged than she had in months. It was a good sign.

For most of her life, she'd endured the toxicity and negativity of her family, specifically her parents and siblings. Moving into adulthood, she'd been forced to set boundaries for her own sanity. Over the years, she'd been able to protect herself from the damaging effects of her family's issues. But the recent close quarters they'd shared as a result of family weddings, significant birthday milestones, and some unfortunate health issues, had shoved those issues back in her face.

After a few incredibly helpful visits with the therapist, she felt a nudge to start writing; to get down on paper all the memories she'd stored for years. And so, began the cathartic process of documenting her life, with a focus on the stories that had brought her the most pain. In releasing the effect of those triggers, she felt a calmness surround her as the weight of those years began to lift.

In just three short months, her first manuscript was complete—twenty chronological chapters of every unsavory and impactful memory she could recall. The exercise of purging these stories in itself was indescribably satisfying. The space they had been renting in her brain felt like the size of a football field. The freedom she felt with their release surprised her the most. If she had any questions at all about how beneficial it had been to spend this much time writing, she threw them all out the window. She had already begun to feel like a new person.

She was proud of this completed work. Although it required some polishing, she was prepared to share her book with some of her closest friends. As she put the word out, the response she received was surprising. She had so many in her network willing to take the time to read and provide her with feedback. As she continued to bask in the new-found calm she'd experienced since putting her pen down, she was in no real rush to proceed.

As she started to hear back, it was ultimately their responses that made her take a huge step back. She had gone deep in her storytelling, no holds barred. Many of the stories were ones her friends hadn't previously been privy to. Some couldn't believe the extent of what she'd endured. Others asked how she could even continue to have contact with her family. But the questions that came most often were the ones that haunted her. What will your family do if you publish this book? How will they react?

Having been so caught up in the act of writing the book and the catharsis experienced as a result, she hadn't really considered the impact publishing might have on anyone, herself included. She did not want her family to experience any negative ramifications as a result of the book. She had been able to dissolve herself of any feelings of bitterness and resentment that she'd previously felt. She now only felt sorry for them.

But of course, they would not see it that way. The thought of purposefully exposing them in a negative light made her a little sick to her stomach. Even if they could never acknowledge it, she knew that every day, they faced their own unresolved issues. She didn't need to exacerbate their misery. She put on the brakes.

At that point in her life, she found herself starting a brand-new job. She knew if she was going to be successful there, she needed to lean in as much as she could without distractions. The manuscript started to collect dust.

As life began to settle, her friends wanted an update. It was then that she shared she'd put the project on hold, unsure about how she could move forward without causing irreparable damage to her family.

Ideas were thrown her way. Write it as fiction. Leave it be. Change all the names. Write it under a pen name. And that was the one that got some traction.

Her thought process kicked into high gear searching for the best pen name. She knew it needed to be meaningful, not simply a name plucked out of thin air. Where to start? So many options. After a few weeks of back and forth, she finally chose a name that felt right. She then started down the path of designing her book cover. She'd confirmed her title during her writing process and felt that a skeleton theme of sorts would be an interesting and eye-catching way to go. She paid a few designers and excitedly waited for their creations to arrive.

Upon receipt of their submissions, if she had to sum up how she felt in one word, that word was *disappointment*. Not a single cover brought her an ounce of excitement. She thought she might gasp in acknowledgement of its perfection when she saw the design that stood out amongst all others. But that feeling completely eluded her. Instead, she reviewed her options with a sense of indifference, doubts starting to swirl in her mind.

Is this what was supposed to happen? Was it really in the cards for her to publish this book? Something wasn't sitting right with her. Perhaps the whole experience of writing her stories down had already served its purpose. Maybe this had just been about her own journey and nothing beyond that. She admitted that the satisfaction she'd experienced upon completion of the manuscript combined with the incredible weight that had been lifted could be representative of all she needed to accomplish. She reluctantly admitted perhaps this was enough. As a result, the manuscript again sat untouched. Months passed.

What she hadn't expected was the continued barrage of questions. Every time she ran into one of her friends, they asked where she was in the publishing process. The questioning was now spanning years. She was so embarrassed about her lack of progress that at one point, she stopped going out in public except for essentials. She didn't want to run into someone who might want a status update.

She couldn't hide forever. Or could she? She had a decision to make. Either put the manuscript aside forever, conceding it was only supposed to be about her own personal journey, or put a plan in place to make some progress.

There was so much information online about publishing a book. Where did she even begin? She had been following a specific author who had published many books of his own and had also helped hundreds of others successfully launch their own books. He was offering complimentary coaching calls for authors looking to publish. She found a convenient time in his schedule and waited excitedly. She had pen and paper ready when her phone rang.

Introductions happened quickly and they got right into the topic of her book. She explained the premise, a chronology of stories highlighting the tough decisions she'd succeeded in making in her life.

He listened intently. He asked great questions. He wondered about her purpose in publishing the book. What goal did she have in mind as she meandered through this maze of a process? She confidently told him she wanted to share her story with the hope that other women who had experienced similar situations would see light at the end of the tunnel.

It was then that he dropped the bomb. "I hate to break it to you," he said, "but nobody cares about your autobiography.

Unless you're already famous, a movie star, have suffered an unspeakable crime that has physically scarred you for life, or any other such newsworthy event, no one cares. Your book won't sell."

Wow, nothing like telling her how he really felt. She wasn't sure if she felt like she'd just been slapped across the face or had a bucket of ice-cold water poured over her.

As she took a minute to regain her composure, she inwardly acknowledged she was talking to someone who had been exposed to publishing hundreds of books versus her experience of publishing none. It only took her a minute to realize she needed to take a deep breath, shake it off, and listen to the free advice he was offering.

He asked more questions about her decision making system and her proprietary app. He wanted to know about the process she used to walk clients through making tough decisions. He said that's the book that will sell one that showcases a process of how to make those types of decisions with confidence. He couldn't express strongly enough that a book focused on helping people and sharing the secret to great decision making would be the right path to follow.

As a decision expert, she had to agree a book like that could lend credence to her profession. She was the poster child of her own five-step decision-making system. Maybe he was on to something. Just before hanging up, he added, "And you need to publish in your own name."

Absorbing his last point, she knew there was a lot to think about. This was one guy's opinion. How much weight was she going to give this isolated conversation? Was she going to let the past forty-five minutes change her course completely?

She didn't feel like it was completely back to the drawing board, but it did feel like two steps forward, ten steps back at this point. She was still inching her way towards the finish line, but she envisioned herself as the slowest tortoise in the pack, stopping to nibble on each blade of grass within eyesight of her path.

Life continued with its full complement of mom, wife, and job duties. The book had once again taken a back burner, but this time in a very productive way. You see, she had always envisioned her brain like a stovetop. She would put some of her most thought-requiring projects on the back burners, where they simmered. When she was finally ready to move them to the front burners, the flavors had burst forth and a full masterpiece had been served. She'd noticed this throughout her life. When she was finally ready to dive in, the product was much further along than when she'd last touched it.

It was no different this time. She decided she would break her chapters out into themes, as many were repeated in the various stories she was sharing. As she cut and pasted piece by piece, the new chapters began to take shape. It was then she realized how one of the biggest challenges she'd face would be replacing every single name. She wanted no ties back to any of the people she'd written about. As the writing continued, she randomly renamed the characters with whatever came to mind. As that exercise progressed, she found herself reviewing the themes that had been uncovered.

There were fifteen in total—an impressive number. As she began the arduous process of re-editing, the newly created lead character of each chapter started taking on a life of her own. Slowly, an idea started percolating. What if she could rewrite her book as a decision expert, walking her clients through each of the tough decisions they'd faced in their lives.

With the pieces coming together, she felt a nudge, reminding her of a fictional novel she'd read in book club years ago. It wasn't the actual story line in *We Need to Talk About Kevin* by Lionel Shriver that had the biggest impact on her. It was the way the story was written and how completely caught off guard she was at the end, when the full story unraveled. With all the books she read since then, it was that one she continued to recommend to friends over and over. The element of surprise had been so compelling for her, she knew wanted to leave her readers with the same feeling.

As she continued to edit chapter after chapter, she portrayed each lead character as a unique woman facing her own hurdles. It would only be in the conclusion where her identity, the silver thread woven through the entire book, would be revealed.

There was just one hiccup. The editing was progressing at a slower than expected pace. Although she had identified specific timelines and enlisted the assistance of an outside editor, a year and a half had gone by without much progress.

Two reasons surfaced for the delay. Even though she hadn't finished the initial editing of all of her own chapters, she'd provided the first five chapters to her editor to review. It was almost a year before those came back. And her editor had been sitting on the next nine chapters for as many months. Something had to give. Typically, she would have tackled the tardiness head on as she wasn't one to shy away from tough conversations. But something was preventing her from pushing any harder in this situation.

As she dug a little deeper, she questioned why things had moved so painstakingly slow. She realized as she dissected the contents of each chapter, she was forcing herself to relive every unsavory event she'd endured in her life. Every time she sat down at her computer, she was transported back to each and every situation she'd tried so hard to put behind her. No wonder it was taking so long. It was like punishing herself all over again. She recalled slamming her laptop shut at one point, having just reread a head-shaking text from a family member. Although she'd spent time working through those issues, reading them in bold print was still a gut-punch to the stomach. Finally acknowledging the cause of a portion of the delay, she managed to give herself some grace.

It still didn't account for her editor's seeming indifference. After a pointed conversation asking about her commitment and other priorities, she determined her editor would not be able to meet the upcoming imminent deadlines. She chose to relieve her of this overwhelming task, allowing her to focus on her own needs and priorities. The result of that decision was a complete separation of an extremely close friendship, but that's for another story. She'd faced a similar circumstance as she was developing her app, The Decision Smith. Her developer had over-promised and under-delivered for a few years before she pulled the plug and found someone who finished it in short order. You'd think she would have learned by now.

She pressed on, determined to find someone who could help her push this project over the finish line. That someone turned out to be right under her nose, her wrangler whom she'd already entrusted with the majority of the operations of her business.

The juxtaposition was incredible. Within four short months, the editing was complete, the cover redesigned, the manuscript ready for upload, the book launch team assembled.

And just like that, *The Decision to Purge – The Year the Skeletons Fell Out of the Closet*, became an overnight #1 and International Bestseller.

• • •

The "she" you've been reading about is me, Dana Peever, The Decision Smith.

One of my greatest passions is helping women make confident decisions that align with the life, business, and relationships they really want.

Making decisions may seem like something you "should" be able to do on your own. But when fears and uncertainty kick in, you can start to waffle and delay. My story is a real-life example of that.

Without knowing how to make big decisions, you can start to put your needs and desires on the back burner (again).

ABOUT THE AUTHOR

DANA PEEVER

Dana Peever is the Creator of The Decision Smith App and The Decision Smith 5-Step System, #yearofyou challenger, #1 Best-Selling Author of *The Decision to Purge – The Year the Skeletons Fell Out of the Closet*, and decision expert at TheDecisionSmith.com.

On top of her zest for life, both her passion and success stem from helping people face their toughest decisions. Having started off pursuing a psychology degree, she ultimately graduated with a Bachelor of Commerce Degree in Human

Resources and Minor in Business Communications from Ryerson University in downtown Toronto, Canada.

Her long and successful career has spanned every level of human resources, but she's never strayed far from her first love of psychology. Mention social or industrial psychology and you'd better pull up a chair—and perhaps a glass of wine.

She lives with her husband and two kids on the shores of Lake Ontario, west of the city.

To celebrate a milestone birthday, she decided it was time to do something for herself after having been on call as a mom and wife for what seemed like forever. The #yearofdana was a resounding success and she has the tattoo to prove it.

Invitation from the Author

Whether you're ready for a purge of your own or simply want to fine-tune your own decision-making skills, I welcome you to start with the www.yearofyouchallenge.com, a FREE five-day reset designed to give you a taste of what can unfold for you when you take full responsibility for living your best possible life. You'll find this and many more resources on my website:

www.TheDecisionSmith.com

Business Name: The Decision Smith

Website: www.thedecisionsmith.com/

Facebook URL: https://www.facebook.com/danapeever

Email: danapeever@gmail.com

"Let your failures be the parts of your journey that build you, not break you."

Keianna Williams

It's January 2012 and I'm walking into the office, with a feeling of anxiety. I know I'm about to make a very important decision - one of the biggest decisions of my life. I could hear the voices in my head: "Keianna what the heck are you doing? You're the Practice Administrator, making a good salary! You have no solid Plan B. You have ZERO dollars in your savings account! Are you sure you want to go through with this?" I take two deep breaths, walk into my boss's office, hand her my resignation letter and, walk out. I did it! I finally built up the courage to fire my boss. I'm finally free! Now I can do what I love to do and pursue my life-long dream of becoming an entrepreneur.

It was the most liberating feeling. I felt like I had been freed from prison. I wasn't sure what lay ahead, but I was ready for it. I knew there were certain people who were going to frown upon my decision to become self-employed because they thought I would fail, but I didn't let them stop me. Deep down inside I knew I was destined for GREATNESS. I was ready to start my wellness coaching and consulting business. I had a great reputation in the health and wellness industry, and I had built great relationships with several holistic doctors in my city. I was confident I would be able to secure coaching contracts with some of those medical offices.

• • •

As my final days of employment were approaching, I was able to secure a three-month contract as a medical consultant for another OB/GYN practice. This was a good sign everything was going to work out.

During the first four years of my business, life was good. I was coaching clients, consulting for medical practices making money and living life on my own terms. It was a dream come true! But as they say, all good things come to an end.

At the end of 2015, my husband and I felt like it was finally time to start a family and begin to plan for it. By April 2016, I found out I was pregnant with twins. This was a big shock. I couldn't imagine my life with two babies. All I could think about was my thriving business. How was I going to stay in business and raise two babies? I had to keep telling myself everything was going to be fine. I was going to keep working until my water broke, pop the twins out, hire a nanny, and go back to work. But reality quickly hit.

My first trimester of pregnancy was horrible. I experienced severe nausea and vomiting day in and day out. I could barely work, but I had to work because if I stopped, I wouldn't make any money. I tried cutting my hours by half and had to drag myself into work three or four days a week. By week twenty I was placed on strict bed rest to prevent preterm labor. I had to terminate all my coaching contracts with the medical offices, as well as the few private coaching clients I had. This was not a part of my grand plan. It was a huge blow and setback. My husband and I were not financially prepared for me to completely stop working, nor were we financially prepared to care for two babies. I began to stress and worry about how we were going to make it.

• • •

The bills quickly began to pile up and our cash reserve was rapidly declining. There weren't many people we could turn to for help because we had "real" bills—two mortgages, two car payments, tens of thousands of dollars in credit card debt, other household bills, business expenses, and two babies on the way.

Creditors began calling and I was doing everything I could to keep up with the payments so I could protect our almost-perfect credit. Our great life was beginning to shatter and the twins had not even entered the world yet. Things were beginning to "get real" for us. At this point I tried to only focus on the health of my babies, but it was a challenge when I had creditors calling me day in and day out.

The morning of October 31, 2016, I remember going in for my routine OB visit and the doctor telling me the frightening news I would have to deliver my twins the next day via c-section. "Wait, what? I'm only at thirty-three weeks! Are my babies going to be okay? C-section? What happened to my natural birthing plan? I'm not ready yet!" The doctor looked at me and told me to calm down and turned to my husband to proceed with the plans for delivery.

At this point I begin to feel like a failure. I had zero business contracts and was generating very little income. My business was falling apart, I was broke, my almost-perfect credit was being ruined, and we were barely making ends meet. Not only did I have to prepare for the arrival of my twins, I also had to figure out how we were going to take care of them. Me getting a job wasn't even an option at this point. To make matters worse, all the stress had begun to take a toll on my marriage.

November 1, 2016 at 5:29 pm my first-born, my son, entered the world, weighing four pounds, six ounces. Three minutes later my princess arrived, weighing three pounds, two ounces. They were tiny, but alive and healthy for the most part. All my stress and worrying had temporarily ceased. All I could focus on were my babies, and of course the pain from my c-section. Three days after delivery, I was discharged to go home, but without my twins who had to stay in NICU for another two weeks.

The morning after I arrived home from the hospital, I remember lying in bed in pain, staring at a stack of bills I had no idea how we were going to pay, thinking about my twins and wondering what happened to my life. I was no longer in control of anything. This was a new place for me. I had always been the one to have a job, money, to make a way out of no way, but this time that wasn't the story. I begin questioning my decision of becoming an entrepreneur. Had I made the right choice? Deep down inside I felt like I did, but it sure didn't look or feel that way. This was supposed to be a time in my life where I was happy, but instead anxiety and depression ruled the day.

• • •

You know how people talk about seeing a light at the end of the tunnel? Let's just say I was at the far end of the tunnel (my downfall) and I couldn't see any light at all.

The eighteen months following the birth of my twins were a nightmare. There I was, stuck at home with two babies, hormones all over the place, unable to care for myself or focus on making money. My business was at a standstill. Meanwhile, my husband was still pursuing his dreams. I started to resent him for it. I was so unhappy while everyone around me seemed to be living their best life. Life seemed so unfair and I began to wonder what I had done wrong to deserve what I was going through. I was battling postpartum depression, I was overwhelmed, exhausted, and stressed out. My husband did not understand my battles. I was ready to walk away from my marriage. I even started to regret having kids. I felt very insecure and worthless. My identity and self-worth were wrapped up in my status, my good credit, my material possessions, and how much money I made. Most of these things had been stripped away from me. I didn't even know who I was anymore. Despite everything I was going through internally and how I felt on the inside, I was able to mask it with a smile on my face in public.

At this point, my husband and I were just co-existing and raising our children. The slightest disagreement would send one of us over the edge. We couldn't even be in the same room most days. I felt so lonely. I was desperate to find someone to talk to but being a very private person made it difficult. Besides, everyone thought I had this perfect life - was I ready to reveal the truth?

I was so broken inside. Some days were so bad that being alive seemed pointless. No matter how hard I tried to make things better, my life continued to spiral downward. I was at my breaking point. I refused to give up on myself, my family, and my business, but I knew things had to change. I liked my coaching business, but I also didn't want to contract with medical offices anymore.

• • •

It's June 2018. I'm lying in a hotel bed alone searching for answers—searching for direction. Earlier that day I had packed my bags and left my husband and kids. I knew if I didn't leave, I was uncertain what would happen. As I lay in that hotel bed, I began thinking to myself, "What happened to the joyful, self-motivated, strong woman I once knew?" I laid in that bed for four days, not turning on the television once. All I had was a notebook and pen. I cried out to God about how unhappy I was with life. I shared with God my dreams and desires for myself, my family, and my business. I no longer wanted to just exist. I wanted to live a joyful, purposeful, and fulfilled life. I wanted my marriage to be restored. I wanted to be the best mom I could be to my twins. I wanted to build my coaching business, but this time I wanted to focus solely on women. I knew God heard my cries. I allowed Him to deal with me and as He spoke, I wrote. I had to do some deep soul searching. It was the most uncomfortable, yet gratifying and eye opening, four days of my life. He began to reveal a lot of things to me about myself. He revealed to me why I was going through what I was going through. It wasn't just about me; it was much bigger than me. He began to show me the thousands of women I would touch through my work.

It was at this point I realized I had to do some serious work on myself inwardly in order to be the best version of me, to be the best mother, to be the woman I was created to be. I knew I had to find happiness within before anything or anyone else could make me happy. I knew I had to learn how to love myself again before I could love my husband and children the way they needed to be loved. To best serve my ideal clients, women who are in search of true happiness and fulfillment, I had to find true happiness and fulfillment myself.

My eyes were opened wide and things started to make sense. My life purpose and vision for my future became noticeably clear.

During my four-day hotel stay, God shed perfect light on the bigger picture. He gave me specific instructions on what I needed to do to make some much-needed changes in my life. It was like He had given me the blueprint, not only for my healing process, but to help others. What I realized was how I had the power to change my situation, to rewrite my story.

• • •

My spiritual journey of healing and self-discovery began immediately the day I returned home from the hotel. I knew it wasn't going to be easy, but I was ready. I began to identify and adjust negative core beliefs. I developed a daily routine of personal time where I prayed, meditated, and focused on personal development. I made a commitment to myself to do this for one hour each day. I also began to practice self-love and self-care. After thirty days I started to notice a difference in my mood and how I was feeling. I was much happier, and it was internal happiness. I had a new outlook on life. I began to appreciate and focus on the things that truly matter, such as my beautiful family, my health, and just being alive. I stopped feeling sorry for myself and stressing over things I couldn't immediately change and started believing things were going to change for the better. My husband noticed a difference and my twins seemed a lot happier. Things were really beginning to turn around.

For the next six months I continued to work on myself personally. While going through this journey of self-discovery, I was also working on rebranding my business and creating a transformation program for women. By the time 2019 arrived, I was a whole, new woman. I was genuinely happy, my relationship with my husband was much better, and I was back to doing what I love--coaching women and transforming lives.

Going through what I went through was a humbling experience. When I look back on my journey, I realize I couldn't have become the woman I am today without going through what I went through. There were plenty of times where I allowed fear and doubt to determine some of the decisions I made. There were plenty of months I didn't make a dime. There is something inside me that will never let me give up. Looking back at what I have gone through and where I am today, I thank God for giving me the tenacity and determination to keep pushing. No one came to save me. I had to make a decision to get up and become my own hero. My struggles became my strength. My test became my testimony.

Today, I am the happiest I have ever been. My marriage is wonderful. My incredible twins are happy and well. Both of our businesses are thriving, and as a result I have financial freedom and time freedom. I'm able to focus my time and attention on the things that are priorities in my life, such as being home with my twins, spending quality time with my family and friends and enjoying every moment of my life. I am living a life I once dreamed of, and I'm on a mission to help as many women as I can to create a life of true joy and fulfillment.

• • •

We all have personal struggles we must deal with. We all have problems and face challenges. It doesn't matter how old or young you are, your education level, how much money you make, or how successful you are. We allow these things to prevent us from living the life we desire. There are key tools you need to apply to your daily lives to truly be happy and live a fulfilling life. And the good news is, we all have the power to change any situation in our life and create the life we desire. The most important step to change anything in life is to first make a commitment to change and believe that we have the power to change.

Everything we want already exists. Oftentimes we're just not in harmony with it. Sometimes we have to ask ourselves what is preventing us from creating the life we desire. More, importantly, we have to ask ourselves if we really want to overcome the challenges. If the answer is yes, we must believe we have the power to manifest the things we want. We must be willing to shift our way of thinking.

Are you living your best life? Are you living a healthy lifestyle? Are you living on purpose and really going after your dreams? Are you truly happy and fulfilled? It's easy to overlook all of the things that contribute to our sense of well-being, nourishment, and fulfillment. Living a healthy lifestyle is not just about the food we eat, but all the factors present in our daily lives, including healthy relationships, a fulfilling career or successful business, regular physical activity, spiritual awareness, a positive mindset, confidence, loving yourself, and taking care of yourself—all of these factors are essential forms of nourishment. The reality is, most people don't know if they are, in fact, living their best life because they haven't done the work to define their best life. It is almost impossible to fulfill your life's purpose and find true success and happiness without first discovering your authentic self, becoming the best version of you, creating a clear vision for your life, and overcoming certain obstacles. It is possible to create the life you truly desire, but it all starts with you!

ABOUT THE AUTHOR

KEIANNA WILLIAMS

Keianna Williams is a Certified Holistic Health and Lifestyle Practitioner, motivational speaker, author, and the Founder and CEO of The Lifestyle Exchange. She has been in the holistic health and wellness industry for more than seventeen years and has worked with holistic doctors and wellness practitioners throughout metro Atlanta. Keianna received her training and certification from the Institute for Integrative Nutrition based in New York City, where she studied over 100 dietary theories, practical lifestyle management techniques, and innovative coaching methods with some of the world's top health and wellness experts.

Keianna also has a degree in Small Business Management with a concentration in Entrepreneurship. Her education and experience have equipped her with extensive knowledge in holistic nutrition, health, and lifestyle coaching. Keianna started The Lifestyle Exchange in 2012 and has helped hundreds of women achieve their health, wellness, and lifestyle goals. Her company offers private, group, and online coaching programs. Her latest program, The Lifestyle Exchange 30-Day Transformation Program has been a huge success. Keianna Williams is passionate about health and wellness, and genuinely believes her life's purpose is to empower and inspire women to become the best version of themselves and create the life they desire.

Invitation from the Author

Visit my website to access a complimentary 30-minute Discovery Session with me to start exploring your dream life!

www.thelifestyleexchange.com

Business Name: The Lifestyle Exchange

Website: www.thelifestyleexchange.com

Facebook URL: https://www.facebook.com/keianna.williams.54/

Email: kwilliams@thelifestyleexchange.com

"The fire is already in you—just add fuel."

Brandi Kowalski

I like to believe I was a unique child, weighing in at just around two pounds, thriving and ready to join the world three months premature. God knew he was going to have his hands full with this girl. A fighter, tenacious, and fashioned to live life by her own rules.

Thinking back over the course of my existence, I don't recall a phase in my life where I haven't overcome some form of self-catastrophe. Physically, emotionally, mentally—we may be genetically inclined to deal with certain vulnerabilities like faulty mood regulation within the brain, medications, medical problems, or even stressful life events. Each has their own trigger points, or length of duration, and sometimes a prescription just won't fix the core problem.

It was the summer of 2001 and I was your typical teenager, inquisitive and bright, and I felt independently minded and willing to rely ultimately on my own insights to guide my initiatives. I was stubborn to the core and desperately seeking an outlet for self-expression as most teenagers do. To others, I was your typical happy teenager on the forefront who thought my siblings were annoying and my parents made me look ridiculous, so I would avoid them at all costs, but on the inside I was an angry teenager—angry with the world and angry with myself.

The air was calm that summer evening as the Tahoe came to a halt in our driveway. The skyline was casting a sunburnt orange over the houses lining our block. The air was still as each of us sat in silence—nobody looking at one other, each staring out the window with a look of despair, all at a loss for words. Time felt frozen as I turned my head and glanced around the vehicle at each of them, remembering the smiles on their faces, hearing the laughter in their voices, each with a distinguished memory as flashbacks from the previous week resonated in my mind. These were beautiful people, full of life, full of love and happiness, and yet there we sat, lifeless, empty, and nothing to say. I was with my then-boyfriend's family, returning home after traveling with them to drop him off at college. The anamorphic feeling came to a halt as his sister glanced at me with a look of helplessness but stern order to press on. Suddenly, piercing the silence amongst us, the father said, "Well" as he reached for the handle on the door and proceeded to the back of the Tahoe to retrieve my luggage.

Sitting in the backseat encompassed by road the trip supplies and necessities every teenage girl must never leave home without, I reached across our mess of chaos and locked eyes with his sister as I wrapped my arms around her and embarrassed the moment. As both of us shed tears of sorrow knowing this might be the last time we see each other, hesitant to talk as we fought back more tears, we leaned in for one final hug as I proceeded to gather myself, grabbed my travel bag, took a deep breath, and reached for the handle of the passenger door.

It was at the exact moment when my feet touched the ground that I felt a shift in my interpersonal alignment, a vortex where my soul and the universe once coalesced now became all jostled and diffused. The affirmation of my vulnerabilities was outlined within me. I felt a sudden wave of apprehension, a heavy uneasy feeling, a deep disconnect within my core that darkened the energy of my spirit. I didn't just lose a friend or a boyfriend that week—I opened a door of altering interpersonal emotions that would affect my life from that point forward. Unable to shake it, I made my way to the back of the Tahoe and retrieved my luggage. Embraced by a monumental moment with these people as they wrapped their arms around me tighter before releasing and making their way on their journey.

Waiting for me patiently was my maternal rock and my foundation at that age, the voice of reason when I struggled with personal conflict. Mother knows best. She could sense the pain across my face, the weight of my shattered heart that evening, as she watched the life light of my spirit fade into the night.

Parts of my character—perception and intuition—were sold to the devil that night as I fell captive to a behavioral condition that consumed my life and opened a floodgate of other problems, leading me down a road of immaturity, instability, and selfishness throughout my teenage years and into young adulthood. Teenagers can be teenagers with typical attitudes and avoidance of their parents, but I made it a habit for self-punishment. College life should be about self-discovery, making friends, and dating. My self-made concoction of co-dependency and depression me indecisive. I experimented with drugs and bounced from one bad relationship to the next. I was a young woman at the age of eighteen who had been raised around the core values of every parent's ideal child, including respect, social aptitude, health and fitness, gratitude, spirituality, love, and selflessness. I came from a well-off family in a loving community surrounded by positive influences, family, and support. And yet I wound up living in a run-down condo in a very poor community with a motley crew consisting of a person who was a tattoo artist by day and drug dealer buy night, his escort of a girlfriend, and my boyfriend at the time who was ten years older than me, bipolar, and convicted of the attempted murder of his estranged wife and two children. Oh, and he was actually still married to her at the time of our relationship.

Manipulation, obedience, and innocence played a major role in my life choices during this time. Whether for money, for rent, for food, or just everyday necessities, hustling wasn't about providing for a family or recognition within an industry—it was about survival. Stealing became an everyday thrill, like a game, for the pleasure of simply never getting caught. But what I failed to realize is that even though I wasn't caught in the moment, I would pay the price of my actions as an adult. Parents instill the life lessons of karma, of choices and decisions having a ripple effect. But when you're young and naïve, the truth behind what your parents tell you carries very little weight. Who was I to believe twenty years down the road I would look back and be horrified at what did with my life and put myself through? At the time, a gang banging ex-convict who was abusive not just physically but mentally and emotionally, was as good as life looked to me for three years. My co-dependency led me down a very dark road of excessive reliance on my boyfriend at the time for approval and a sense of identity.

Clarity came rarely, but when you come from a good home, raised by a loving family, knowing the difference between what's acceptable and what's grounds for being disowned, when that line in the sand is drawn between comfort and comfortable, sometimes your family has to stop having any contact with you at all because of the choices you're making. I like to believe there is engrained within our morals and values a core belief that leaves one filled with a sense of realization of the one person who truly matters at heart. It takes a lot of strength and courage to climb out of what feels like an endless hole. For me, fear played a major factor. Fear for my family, fear for my friends, but fear for my life and my future. That burst of realization had me yearning for a future free from a lifestyle I didn't want to be a part of any longer.

Since I was a child I have dreamed of a big, bold, lifestyle—glamorous and lively, nothing conforming me to the small town I grew up in, tucked away in the corn fields of Nebraska, the black hole of the United States. I needed opportunity. I needed options. Whether this stems from co-dependency and self-identify I don't exactly know, but I knew I wanted a fresh start, a clean slate. It was often a topic of discussion for me on a daily basis. Whether I ran out of dreams to talk about or my coworkers were tired of hearing about my goals, someone blatantly asked me one day, "Why don't you just move?" Dumbfounded and speechless, I found myself questioning why I didn't do exactly that. This one simple question seemed to resonate with me. I found myself laying a map across my desk with the intention of selectively choosing a new life by the drop of a pen. With my co-worker best friend by my side, my stomach was turning. My nerves were in overdrive, as though someone was forcing me to choose at this exact moment the direction my life would take. It was the beginning of March in 2007, and all it took was one drop of ink on a map and an eighteen-hour non-stop drive with whatever would fit in my car, encompassed by nothing but brown dry desert, one of the hottest places you could possibly live, for me to find myself and discover what my livelihood depends on.

However, like most of us, I am a creature of habit and often choose to do the same thing rather than try new and different things. So, even though I found myself living in a new state (Arizona), surrounded by new faces and new opportunities, it didn't take long for my co-dependency and good ol' side kick of depression to nestle itself back into the core of my life. I found myself once again involved in a bad relationship, filled with instability, lacking purpose and direction, and worst of all, steeped in jealousy—the two-faced side to my co-dependency. I can't say it was always bad, as every relationship has its moments. Something between us seemed to be working because our relationship lasted eight years.

You have to wonder, how does one end up in that kind of position, making those kinds of choices in life that lead down such paths? Co-dependency is an emotional and behavioral condition that affects an individual's sense of identity through an excessive reliance on or need for approval from someone. It is a disorder of a "lost self." A codependent loses their connection to their innate self. Instead, their thinking and behavior revolves around a person, substance, or process. They struggle to have healthy, mutually satisfying relationships, and oftentimes form emotionally destructive and/or abusive relationships, whether that be with friends, family, or romantic partners.

It was understanding this that made me realize why my luck hardly ever changed, why the accidents just became more amplified and how I was substituting one bad habit for another. Then in 2008 I was diagnosed with pre-cancerous cervical cancer and endometriosis, which came as a shock to me when they started talking about a full hysterectomy before I had even considered the possibility of a family at the age of twenty-two. I did have surgery to treat my pre-cancerous condition but said no to the suggested hysterectomy.

Then in January of 2010 I found myself standing in an airport staring at that same man with only the clothes on my back and two large suitcases filed with my most precious and personal belongings in the state of New Hampshire, once again questioning whether I had made the right decision. He had left Arizona for New Hampshire for a job opportunity, and I followed six months later.

From the deserts of Arizona to the forests of New England, although older, seasoned with culture and an appreciative understanding for my past choices in life, I knew where I wanted to be. The problem was understanding how to get there, especially trying to figure it out between two co-dependent individuals. By the fall of 2010 I was diagnosed with PCOS (polycystic ovarian syndrome), and by 2012 I underwent my second major surgery. From health conditions and natural disasters, evictions and financial ruin, it only took four years for the destruction and chaos to surface. Though my only baggage was my personal health, the weight of the Jealousy led to fighting, which opened the gateway to drugs and alcohol that left me in a mental state of constant anxiety and fear. I was physically ailing myself with low self-esteem and self-worth. I resorted again to fear—fear for my life and my future, and once again the realization ignited inside. I knew this wasn't *it* for me.

Life has never really stood in my way. I am a free bird. I have grown a deep passion for and love of travel. I've learned to be very optimistic, though some would say unrealistic. I stay more or less hopeful. I believe the universe guides us in directions in life that will fulfill our personal attributes. However, it's up to us to believe in that path and actually do something with it. By the summer of 2014 I had once again concluded my self-worth to the confines of my two-door, black cherry Nissan Altima, aka cherry berry, the car that has been with me through the Hail Mary of my life—driving back to Arizona, knowing I was NOT going to move again. Arizona would become my place to call home, this time with every intention of a fresh start. I made a vow to myself I was going to get help and do right by *me* this time. I started over at ground zero with the just the clothes in my car, $1,300 to my name, a bottom-of-the-barrel leasing agent position in the multi-housing industry, and a small two-bedroom apartment with nothing but freshly laid carpet to sleep on until I could afford the finer necessities to furnish my new home.

Finally, at a place in life where my soul and the universe could once again coalesce, I felt things were starting to fall into place. I was working, seeking counseling, and even meticulously choosing who was deserving of my time and energy. With all things positive in motion, I found myself in love with the man who would soon become the father to my child and support system throughout life. Every couple goes through the honeymoon stage, but ours was more like a honeymoon trip as it was abruptly ended when I was struck with extensive vision problems in the fall of 2014. Our relationship was either going to sink or flourish at this point, either way it was in fate's hands. From keratitis to ulcers on my corneas and three long months of minimal vision (sight is a gift many take for granted until you cannot see), it was an overall embarrassing time in my life, but the worst part of it all was the not knowing—never knowing if I would ever see the world in such a beautiful light again. Following various tests and medications, I was finally diagnosed with an autoimmune disease called Lupus, and secondary disease called Sjogren's, both of which explain all the underlying female issues and health troubles I'd been having. My luck didn't stop there! Six months after being diagnosed with an autoimmune disorder, I continued to have residual problems that lead to the discovery of degenerative arthritis, as well as a herniated disc that lead to a spinal fusion in 2020 during the midst of the novel coronavirus and COVID-19 pandemic.

At the time I never really understood why everything was happening, how I would get through it, or what the future would look like for me. There has always been a passion for entrepreneurship and the flexibility to tend and care for a family as well as myself given all my health complications, but because of my "lost self," I struggled with finding a niche that suited those desires within me. eBay, Beachbody, Etsy—those only give back about as much as I put in, and I can honestly say I was never whole-heartedly committed, and though the intention and the energy were there, the passion, the drive, the hunger was not, so I would give up and move on to the next conquest.

The one thing I came to realize was how the change had to come from within me. The drive had to be there. The co-dependency and depression could be a façade for only so long before the truth of the matter came to light, I had to find the hunger inside me to fuel the climb out of a lifestyle of chaos and destruction. This flame was ignited in the fall of 2017 when I brought my very first, beautiful, healthy baby girl into this world. To love and care for another being is one of the greatest joys and yet also the worst pain I will ever experience, all wrapped into a tiny body that I only hope to raise in every aspect of physical, emotional, social, and intellectual development to excel on every level beyond me. Without a doubt, I can honestly say I have been successful at being a parent. Settling for good is better than striving for perfection, although I believe I am perfect for my family, and I love them all beyond all reason.

It has taken twenty years for my soul and the universe to unite in an energy conducive to healing and mending my life's wounds, realigning my stars, and lighting the path to clarity and success for me both personally and professionally. In August 2019 at a conference in Atlanta for my better half, I was introduced to and befriended by a young woman who shared the same interests and passions in life, love, and success. Presented with a feeling of encouragement, devotion, and much appreciation, I was acquainted with a rare opportunity to open a franchise and grow a marketing firm on the West Coast. By the end of September that year, I decided to take a leap of faith, as everyone does when a flame inside is ignited. I was up at all hours of the night brainstorming and mapping my methodical plan for success with Luxe Solutions, an entity my better half and I have forged into a consulting business. With the founding of Luxe Solutions, I became a franchise owner of Arizona-based Savvy Marketing West Coast, the west coast office of Savvy Marketing Agency based in Jacksonville Florida. I oversee sales and strategy, catering to all the west coast clientele and operations to assist clients in developing a solid foundation for their business through marketing and advertising.

I couldn't tell you if it was fate or if I just needed a nudge from my subconscious the moment we were blessed with a beautiful mini me, but the universe has certainly blessed me with the chance to redeem myself. It wasn't just about a choice for me, but a lifestyle change aligned with my deepest inner being, a need to be fulfilled on multiple levels. I found my path in life and have surrounded myself with a loving, caring support network of friends and family. I have a beautiful family, a place to call home, and have successfully indulged in a lifelong goal I set out in search of since my younger days. I can't say every day is easy as my depression still creeps up on me every now and then, but I have learned to let go of my codependency. I have learned to love myself, accept my faults, and live my life in a way that makes me happy every day I walk this earth. You don't have to have a recovery story or a success in life to find growth and development within you, you just have to find what fuels yourself to building a better you.

ABOUT THE AUTHOR

BRANDI KOWALSKI

B randi Kowalski is a Lifestyle Coach, WAHM (work-at-home-mom), and Founder of Luxe Solutions & Franchise Owner of Savvy Marketing West Coast. She is a management professional with an extensive background in business marketing and management. She is deeply familiar with contract negotiation, client development, and is experienced in web development and promotional planning. Brandi holds an associate degree in Video/Audio Communications, a bachelor's degree in Marketing and Advertising, a master's degree in Business Management, and is a certified Digital Marketing Strategist, specializing in social media management and Digital Cinematography.

In 2014 Brandi became a bonus mom to two beautiful children. Then in the fall of 2017 Brandi had her very own beautiful baby girl. In 2019 Brandi founded Luxe Solutions to assist entrepreneurs in accelerating the growth of their businesses. The following year, Brandi joined Savvy Marketing Agency based in Jacksonville Florida and became a franchise owner of Savvy Marketing West Coast based in Arizona. Brandi and her team of experts from around the globe provide digital marketing and creative services to agencies, franchises, and medium-sized businesses. In her spare time, she runs a small Etsy business and still manages to enjoy the sun and spend time with her three beautiful children and her husband, Brandon.

Invitation from the Author

Visit my website to access a FREE Online Presence Health Check for your business:

https://savvyagency.com/west-coast/

Business Name: Luxe Solutions

Website: https://savvyagency.com/west-coast/

Facebook URL:
https://www.facebook.com/savvymarketingwest/

Email: brandi@savvyagency.com

"As the CEO of your life, you make the rules and you run the show. Own it and go get what you really want."

Diana Mantey

"**S**o, are you going to resign, or do you want me to fire you?"

"When do I have to let you know?" I asked.

"Now. Like this minute."

Welcome to the most unexpected Thursday-after-five-pm conversation of my life.

Entangled in feelings of shock, overwhelm, embarrassment, fear, and deceit, I made the decision to quit. In hindsight, I should have let them fire me!

The Assistant Director position I had worked so hard for was gone, just like that.

It was the position for which I invested three years into getting a master's degree—the position I manifested for months—the position everyone on my team said I was "perfect for."

I felt like I had been punched in the stomach, with the wind knocked out of me and hoping I was just living a bad dream.

But I wasn't.

As I drove home on that surprisingly cool June evening, I sobbed endlessly, barely able to clearly see the road ahead. And as those salty tears streamed down my face as I drove down the highway, a serene feeling of relief overcame me. I realized I never had to go back to the place that had me dreading Mondays and filled me with the kind of anxiety that made it nearly impossible to unclench my fists. And with that thought I smiled, thinking maybe, just maybe I had been given the greatest gift I never asked for.

When I pulled into the dark garage, I wiped my tears and exhaled big breaths before heading inside to tell Nick my fate. He understood, like I knew he would.

We spent the evening laughing and cooking one of our favorite dinners—radish cakes with bean sprouts—like nothing in the world was wrong. And as night fell and the moon rose bright, Nick hugged me a little tighter than usual and reassured me everything was going to be okay.

Being twenty-seven, perfectly able, and jobless is not a good look. I knew I was talented. I knew I was competent—I could learn how to do just about anything. I was confident the job search wouldn't take long. I gave myself a month, and that month passed by quickly with nothing to show for it.

I was applying for basically every open position in my field, with slow progress being made. I'd tickle with excitement each time I received an email invitation to interview. But I knew first-hand (from being on way too many hiring committees) that the interview and hiring process could take anywhere from four to six months, so nothing was going to happen any time soon.

In the meantime, I was applying anywhere and everywhere I could find an online application or places hosting in-store hiring events.

Crickets.

I'd still love to know the *real* reason why no gas station, fast food restaurant, or ice cream parlor would hire me.

"Overqualified" is what was insinuated over and over again.

Maybe they were also skeptical of the fact I was applying to work at their establishment when the "Diana" on paper looked like she should be doing so much more.

But I wasn't.

I needed a job, and I was starting to feel desperate.

In the meantime, I read a lot. I hit the gym nearly every day with the morning crowd. I became quite a good "housewife" and my cooking repertoire really expanded. Pad Woon Sen, anyone?

But I was antsy, unfulfilled, and eager to start feeling useful again, not to mention needing to start making some cash!

And the more I applied to jobs and got rejected while living a life of such freedom, the more I questioned if I really wanted to go back to 'work' in the traditional sense.

Yeah, I know—does anybody *really* want to go to work? If work were optional, I think ninety-nine percent of us would opt out. Well, maybe not, and for those of you who wouldn't, congratulations on finding your true calling and passion!

So, as I mindlessly scrolled through my newsfeed one hot August afternoon, an ad popped up about a webinar on how to make money from anywhere by creating an ad agency.

Juicy, right?

I clicked, registered for the next one, and felt such joy writing something on my calendar that I felt in my heart could be my big breakthrough. I was hyped to learn what this could be about. I had some experience with social media marketing and content creation from my previous positions, so I knew this was something I could definitely do, as long as it was legitimate.

And legit it appeared to be! I purchased the $997 program that said it would teach me how to create a six-figure advertising agency in a year!

I quickly made this advertising agency course my new obsession. My days consisted of BodyPump workouts, DoorDash deliveries to make some cash, and studying and implementing the course. I was on top of the world, even though my income was less than a college student's. Every day, I was learning something new, practicing it, and refused to stop until I completely understood and perfected it. My new normal was ten-hour days of DoorDashing and building a business most people thought was a complete joke. I did my best to ignore them. To combat their criticism, I recorded a video and posted it on social media declaring I would make $100k in 2020 for all to see and hold me accountable.

One September afternoon, the phone rang. It was a job offer—a work-from-home Assistant Director position with a $70,000/year salary. I couldn't believe it. It sounded like a complete dream, with a salary tens of thousands more than I had ever been paid before. I accepted the position in the moment, thankful for the opportunity to have consistent income again. But when I hung up, my stomach sank, and I instantly felt regret. It wasn't what I wanted. I loved the business I was starting, and I knew in my heart I had to see it through, or I'd always wonder, "What if?"

When Nick got home from work that evening, I told him about the job offer and he congratulated me and emphasized how accepting the job was the responsible and practical thing to do.

"You can do advertising on the side," he said.

But I knew that to get my business off the ground and have any success with it would require much more than a couple hours a day. At the same time, I also knew this accepted job offer of mine was a relief for him. He had been relentlessly supporting me financially, emotionally, and mentally over the past three months, and I could tell he was tired. I agreed that taking the job was the right choice.

As my start date crept closer and closer, I continued to commit every waking hour to my business so I could make as much progress as possible before having to demote it to a "part-time hobby." I hated the thought of going back to work, so I almost ignored it was happening and reveled in the freedom lifestyle I had grown to adore.

Anxiety and resentment built up, and the weekend before my start date, I had to make a confession. I told Nick I didn't want to go back to work, and as anyone would expect, we argued. I could understand every point he made about how I was being completely insane, living in some unrealistic dream world, asking what my plans were for making any kind of real money. Each point was so valid and real, but they couldn't deter me from this vision I had for my life—our life—and I knew I could bring it to fruition if I was given this chance. As I explained and expressed this to him, our guards came down and he agreed I could quit the job I hadn't even started yet to pursue some wild passion that had absolutely no guarantee.

"You have twelve months to make this work," he said.

"Okay, I get it," I replied.

We made a deal, hugged it out, and on Monday morning I called my would-be supervisor, told her I would no longer be starting that week, apologizing profusely and explaining my heart was in a different place. She wished me all the luck in the world, and when I hung up the phone, I realized how shit just got real.

I continued spending my days DoorDashing (which got quite draining and monotonous) and progressing through the course at lightning speed, feeling confident I was nailing the tactics and set-up, getting ready to rock and roll. All I needed were clients. And I needed them ASAP.

When I arrived at the pricing module, I was thrown for a complete and unexpected loop. The course was based on the ability to close at least three clients on a $2,997 monthly retainer rate to hit the six-figure mark. Reading that rate burned holes through my eyes. I could barely look at the number, let alone believe I was expected to ask somebody for that much money in exchange for advertising services and think they would say "Yes."

$2,997 was more than the monthly paycheck I was accustomed to receiving for my nine-to-five work. $2,997 was the amount I would budget for a trip to Asia. $2,997 would look great in my 401K! I refused to believe any sane person would pay $2,997/month for advertising services, regardless of how many other students in the program were getting clients to say "yes" and were well on their way to six-figure goal.

But I also refused to pity myself. I knew this was my own mental block—one I had to choose to overcome or I would have to find my own way to success that felt true and authentic to me.

So naturally, I started working for free (even though I was barely surviving off my DoorDash income). I'd network and do outreach like crazy, as uncomfortable as it was, just for the chance to get on a Zoom call with someone and teach them how to set up their ads or optimize them—at no cost. I was convinced I was doing myself a favor by establishing credibility and providing massive value upfront, and maybe these people might actually consider paying me in the future. As it turned out, most had no real interest in a long-term relationship.

Out of a raw necessity to survive and financially contribute more to our household, I started charging for my services. Thirty dollars per hour is what I decided on, and it still felt uncomfortable, as if it was too much. I was thrilled every time I landed an hourly consultation, and the payment came through. For me, it signified that for every thirty dollars I made online, I could eliminate two hours of DoorDashing that week AND that I was making progress in my business, which I celebrated like it was my birthday each time.

I slowly got up the courage to ask for a monthly fee for my services. It started at $250, then $500, then $750 and even $800. A "good month" for me in my business was $2,000 (before subtracting business expenses) and an additional $1,200 from DoorDash. It was about the same as the monthly nine-to-five paychecks I would have received, so I rationalized I was doing well.

But I wanted more. And to hit the $100k goal I declared, I needed more.

Social media is an amazing and evil thing. It keeps us connected, provides the ability to make mad money with a WiFi connection, and yet it is the place we as humans end up going to "relax" or "pass time," which typically ends in serious comparison mode and feelings of inferiority.

I saw (and still see) so many people winning online. Making six and seven figures in a month. Making four and five figures in a day. I couldn't fathom how they were doing it. What did they know that I didn't? How do I become THEM?

I quickly realized I needed to hire a coach—a good coach who had achieved what I wanted to achieve. I knew it was going to be about a $3,000 investment, which was certainly money I didn't have just lying around, but I knew it was where I needed to invest so I could grow and figure out what the hell I was missing in my business that all these other successful people had. So I joined a ton of groups, observed from afar, and had two hot contenders to hire, but I just couldn't get myself to raise my hand and say, "I'm in!" Something didn't feel totally aligned, so I continued to hold out.

The momentum I had in my business was like a rollercoaster and I was on an income hamster wheel, supplementing my ten-hour workdays with nights and weekends filled with DoorDashing just to make ends meet. I was stressed, moody, and exhausted. The fact I couldn't figure out how to make things work on my own made me feel like a failure. I reeked of imposter syndrome and tried my best to outwardly mask the lack of confidence haunting me inside. I cried a lot. I was grossly undercharging and couldn't get larger numbers to even come out of my mouth on sales calls out of fear of rejection. I promised Nick I would make this work, and I was committed to figuring it out. I was going to make $100k in 2020, even though Nick said he would be proud of me if I made $35k—thanks, love!

When COVID-19 practically shut down the USA (and world) in March 2020, I was finally getting my brand and market positioning on track (or so I thought) and was consistently hitting my $2k months, which I felt good about, but was by no means what I was going to settle for.

In late March, I saw a post on my newsfeed from a coach I knew was crushing it in her business about a free workshop her coach was hosting. I immediately commented and said I wanted in. The closer I could get inside the mind and communities of successful entrepreneurs, the more I knew I would grow.

The workshop was everything I needed in my life and more. Talk about a fire being lit under my butt—it contained massive, free value and I experienced so many small and immediate wins in just a week. My confidence was reignited. As the workshop host pitched her $18,000 coaching program at the end, I was immediately intrigued, but figured I wasn't on a high enough level to have success in the program, nor did I have any idea how I could afford that investment.

Over the weekend, Nick and I were taking a walk around our neighborhood when I decided to tell him about this $18,000 coaching program. He knew I wanted to hire a coach but asked me if I really needed an $18,000 coach or if I could start out with a four-figure coach.

A valid question.

A five-figure coaching investment could be risky, but also insanely worth it. And as much as I thought I was too elementary to join, it also felt like the place I was meant to be.

I brought it up nearly every day after, hoping he might change his mind and agree to let me sign up and that taking on this type of credit card debt made sense. The day enrollment to the program was closing, I made my final pitch to Nick, coupled with cute puppy dog eyes and a begging plea, which he basically couldn't resist, so he agreed I could enroll. His sign-off was so important to me because he is the most rational, analytical person I know, and for it to feel "right", I needed him to be onboard. I threw our credit cards down in the final hours, too excited to sleep and hoping I hadn't just made a really stupid decision. Shit just got real, again.

Turns out, joining the coaching program was one of the absolute best decisions of my life, and I made back my investment in the first three months. I joined a community and network of unstoppable, kickass entrepreneurs who are relentless in their pursuit, experts at what they do, and committed to their vision, which is the same entrepreneurial path I am on, too. Within seven months of implementing the strategies and methods I learned, I hit $100k in my business! I did it! It did come at a cost, of course—countless ten-plus-hour workdays, weekends spent on the computer, Nick's undeniable love and support, investing over $35k in coaching, mentorship, and training, immense moments fear and discomfort (especially when being coached to raise my damn price—dramatically), yet always trusting the process and moving in faith, even when I didn't know exactly where I was going.

Now, I am actively building a global brand grounded in authenticity, transparency, and whole-hearted client care, which requires me to be real and embrace all of who I really am—including my flaws and my past.

I'll admit, I feel I've lived letting my history and other people's words and perspective define me and what I can accomplish, which has held me back, kept me playing small, and caused me to self-sabotage and feel judged if I publicly share my experiences and successes.

So, with this chapter, I sovereignly declare I am done living in the shadows! I exist to live a big, beautiful, and meaningful life, and I will contribute more to the world than I receive in return.

And I want you to know *you* can have all this, too, if you want it bad enough.

I wasn't born knowing I was going to be an entrepreneur. I didn't believe in the power of manifesting until I realized my manifestations came true. I had no idea how everything was going to work out—all I knew was that I had the drive and fighting spirit to do whatever it took. And I'm nowhere near done yet.

So now it's your turn. What would you do if you escaped the shadows? What dream or mission is living in your heart, in your gut, that you know YOU need to bring to life so you can change lives, make an impact, and create a legacy?

Whatever it is, go act on it—today. I'll always believe small progress is the best progress, and that the best investment you can make is in yourself. So if it's money that is holding you back from chasing your dream, here's a piece of advice: Quit buying expensive coffee, burritos, and shoes, and start saving and investing in your dream (and DoorDashing).

If you're facing a hard time, feeling like you've hit rock bottom, where is the silver lining in your experience you can turn into the greatest gift you never asked for?

You're the CEO of your life—you decide what you make of it. You make the rules, you run the show. Live with #noexcuses and #noregrets!

ABOUT THE AUTHOR

DIANA MANTEY

Diana Mantey is a Facebook™ Ads Launch Strategist who specializes in targeted lead generation for aspiring seven and eight-figure service-based business owners. From accumulating years of experience in service-based sales and marketing, Diana brings a fresh perspective to every advertising campaign and strategy. With a thorough understanding of the buyer and their journey, Diana is able to create highly optimized ad campaigns that lead to inspiring client results.

Diana has been trained, mentored, and coached by some of the leading digital marketers and entrepreneurs in the online space, and grew her practice to over six figures in revenue within her first year in business. Diana currently resides in Tempe, Arizona, with her partner, Nick.

Invitation from the Author

Visit my website to learn more about how you can use Facebook ads to crush your next launch!

www.ngadvertising.com

Business Name: NG Advertising

Website: www.ngadvertising.com

Facebook URL: https://www.facebook.com/dmantey/

Email: diana@ngadvertising.com

"We all have to weather storms in life. Just remember, without the rain there would be no rainbow."

Louise Feltham

What are you doing? Are you going to spend the rest of your life like this? This is not about you anymore. You need to get out of here. NOW. It is 2016 and these words are going through my head as my daughter cries in my arms and tells me she doesn't want to be here anymore. I have been living with this anxious sick feeling for years now. There is something "off," but I can't put my finger on it. It feels wrong but it's not about me anymore.

I've dreamed of my fairytale wedding since I was twelve. We would marry in a Church, I would be wearing a white wedding gown, and the fragrance of white roses would fill the air. As we vow to love, honor, and obey each other in front of our friends and family, he would stare lovingly into my eyes. It was perfect.

This couldn't be further from my fairytale though. But, for you to understand how I ended up here, I must take you back ten years…

It is the Summer of 2006 in Melbourne, Australia. My name is Charlotte, I am twenty-seven years old and I still have the hint of a South East London accent. It always gets thicker when I've had a few drinks and that is exactly what got his attention that warm Melbourne night.

"English, right?" he asked me, in his thick Australian accent. "Yeah, how did you know?" I replied, not realizing my Australian accent had faded. Martin laughed and invited me to join him and his friends, Peter and Lucy, at the other table. It was nice to have someone pay me some attention, even if he was the total opposite of my usual type. He was kind, polite, and seemed into me so I thought "what the hell." We spent the night drinking and chatting until closing. At the end of the night he asked me if he could call me the next day. I gave him my phone number and I left with my friends. It was a bit of fun, but I had already friend-zoned him in my mind.

I didn't know it back then, but ten years later I would be living in another city, married to this man, with three children and fearing for my life.

It's early November and my period is late. I'm holding a pregnancy test in my trembling hand and I can't tell if I'm excited or scared. Martin is out drinking with his mates—a common occurrence these days. I'm standing in the bathroom on my own as I wait for what feels like three hours for the second line that I know is coming. I'm pretty sure I know what his reaction will be and when he returns from the pub that evening with a can of Rum in his hand. I know this is not going to go well. "You'd better sit down and put that drink down," I said to him. My voice shaking. "I'm pregnant," I blurted out as if I was vomiting out the words. He just looked at me and picked up the can and continued drinking before replying "Okay, what now then?"

I was thirty weeks pregnant when I realized he was cheating on me. I could hear his Nokia phone going off constantly. Beep-beep, beep-beep. Over and over again. It wasn't unusual for him to text a few of his mates back and forth but this was different. This was nonstop and I sensed secrecy. I could feel the paranoia in the air. There was something he did not want me to know. He took his phone with him tightly gripping it in his hand as he walked to the bedroom and put it face down on his side of the bed.

I followed him and picked up the phone after he had closed the door to the bathroom and searched through the recent messages. My heart stopped. I knew already, before I even read the message at the top, what the contents were. Every message was from and to Chloe. I had noticed recently when we had been at his friend John's house that Martin and Chloe had been suspiciously friendly. I brushed it off at the time, yet now in the middle of my bedroom with the sound of the shower in the background, it all became clear. I felt sick, not like morning sickness, this was deeper. A feeling of complete dread washed over me. I was drowning. I started to panic. "What will I do, how am I going to raise this baby on my own?" I thought to myself.

My mind was racing a million miles an hour as I heard the shower turn off and suddenly, he was there in front of me. "What's going on with Chloe?" I asked him as I thrust his phone in his hand. He laughed. That same laugh I had heard that first night we had met. Except this time, he wasn't laughing *with* me, he was laughing *at* me. "It's nothing. We're just friends. You know that." My gut was telling me what my heart already knew. He had been seeing her behind my back. But my mind didn't want to believe he would do that to me while I was pregnant with his child. "What if he's telling the truth? Are you *really* going to make yourself a single mum over this? What if you're wrong? What about the fairytale ending?" Sure, I could leave, but what kind of life would I have? "Who is going to want a single mum with a kid? If you leave now, you can forget your fairytale" I thought. "No, I can make this work," I told myself. "Sorry," I replied. "It must be the hormones," and that was the last time we ever spoke about Chloe.

I thought once the baby was here our relationship would improve, and for a while it did, but I desperately wanted to get married to complete my fairy tale. Every time I had to take my daughter to an appointment, I could feel the judgement when the receptionist assumed, we had the same surname. It was seven years before he finally proposed after much begging on my part and the event was nothing like I had pictured in my mind. Regardless, I was emotionally invested and there was no turning back. I spent the next twelve months planning the wedding, and with each task that got ticked off the list it was getting harder and harder to pull out. I knew this wasn't right, but I kept thinking once we were married this feeling in the pit of my stomach would disappear.

As I woke up on that sunny February morning in 2013 I was overcome with excitement. I wasn't nervous like I thought I would be. It was pure excitement. As I walked down the aisle with the biggest smile on my face, I felt nothing but love for Martin. It was all going to be okay. All the other stuff was behind us. It was the perfect day, and everything was *almost* exactly as I had imagined it in my mind. I was finally married!

I became pregnant again soon after the wedding. Twelve months after our wedding I gave birth to our second daughter. As our second daughter turned one, I could tell the stress of two children was getting to him. He was angry a lot. I found myself taking on more and more responsibility with the kids, to keep him from getting stressed.

I wasn't feeling supported or loved. We were going through the motions. "Maybe it's me," I thought. "If I try harder to please him and be attentive then maybe I can make it work. Yep, that's the answer. I need to try harder. I need to cut him some slack." My mind continued trying to search for ways to make sense of this. "It's not normal to feel this way about your husband. There must be something seriously wrong with me. I have everything I've always wanted but I'm still not satisfied. It's me," I resolved.

The relationship continued to deteriorate following the birth of our third child, a son, but I convinced myself to settle. "It's not really that bad. I'm the problem," I kept telling myself. "We need counselling," he said. "Maybe you should go and see a doctor? Maybe you need to see a psychologist or a counsellor? Maybe there's something wrong," he told me. He sounded concerned. I had noticed how my mental health was declining. He had a point. "It must be the postnatal depression again," I stated matter-of-factly. After all, this wasn't the first time. It's not surprising it would happen again. A week later I saw my regular doctor. I was diagnosed with postnatal depression and anxiety and prescribed medication. I tried to verbalize how I was feeling but I couldn't really put it into words. I didn't feel he understood - hell, I didn't even understand it. "I think the psychologist will help," he said and handed me the mental health care plan he had written.

Martin drove me to my first appointment and as I got out of the car, he said to me "Don't forget to tell them *everything*." I poured my heart out about feeling depressed and anxious, but the psychologist seemed more interested in talking about my husband. She asked me a lot of questions about his behavior. I found myself wanting to protect him and making excuses for him. Something inside of me kept whispering, "Don't tell her *that*." I wanted to blurt out *everything* like Martin had said, but I was scared. I couldn't tell her I was feeling suicidal some days. What if she contacted the Department of Child Safety? Would they take my children away? I had to keep swimming. "Does he yell directly at you or the children?" asked the psychologist. I remembered what Martin had said in the car. "Yes," I answered. "Does he ever throw or break furniture or other property?" Again I answered, "Yes." I knew what was coming. "Please just say the words," I thought. "What you are experiencing is domestic violence," she said. A wave suddenly washed over me, but this time it wasn't sickness or anxiety. This time I felt completely calm. For the first time in years I had mental clarity.

I walked out of the psychologist's office feeling like a weight had been lifted and I didn't mention the card I had hidden in my bag. The psychologist had given me the details to a service called DV Connect. I would call them on Monday when Martin was at work.

I woke up on Monday feeling better than I had felt in years. I'm sure Martin must have noticed something had changed in me. I was excited but scared. Once I made this call there was no turning back. This was it. After Martin left for work, I waited for the hour hand to reach 9:00 am on the clock in the kitchen. Tick, tick, tick, tick. It felt as though time was going by in slow motion. In my journal on the kitchen bench I had neatly written the following bullet points.

- Husband yells, screams, and swears at me and the kids every day.

- Children and I are scared.
- Drinks at least six beers every night.
- Feel like I'm walking on eggshells all the time.
- Punched a hole in the wall and threw a baby swing across the room.
- Very angry. Worried about what he will do next.

I dialed the number and as the lady on the other end of the phone began running through some questions, I felt that sick feeling rising again. She asked me some basic questions and told me she would be referring me to a domestic violence service. I felt my blood pressure rising. I didn't want to be passed from one person to another, I just wanted help *now*. As I put the phone down, I felt helpless again. All I could do was wait for the phone to ring.

Later in the day as I was walking through the center of town my phone rang. I looked down. It was a private number. I knew instantly. This is it. I felt a wave of panic wash over me, drowning me again. There were people everywhere. I could hear the blur of voices melding into one muffled noise. "I don't think I can do this," I said to myself. The lady on the other end of the phone spoke to me in a soft and compassionate tone. Her name was Sarah. "You're so brave for reaching out. You can do this," she reassured me, and in that moment, nothing else mattered except her voice. She was my lifeline. I listened intently as she asked me a lot of personal and deep questions I answered as best I could. She encouraged me to give every last detail no matter how small and so I did. Things that had seemed inconsequential at the time suddenly screamed warning bells at me. "How had I not seen just how serious this was?" I questioned. It didn't make sense.

At the end of the phone call, Sarah explained to me I would be referred to a more local domestic violence service for crisis counselling so I would be better equipped to leave safely. Although I could now see the severity of the situation, I still didn't consider myself to be in crisis. Regardless, I went along with what she said. I trusted her.

A few days after the phone call, I found myself in the office of my assigned crisis counsellor. "I'm going to ask him to leave so the kids and I can stay in the house," I stated matter-of-factly. "Okay," replied Marie, "but what if he doesn't leave?" I assured her with, "I'm sure he'll do the right thing. He wouldn't kick the kids out on the street."

The following week as I was standing in the loungeroom of our home Martin said to me, "You want to leave, you leave. The kids can stay with me. This is your problem not theirs."

"Shit," I thought. "This has totally backfired."

I had already packed a bag of emergency things in preparation and so the kids, one bag, and I arrived at my mum's house. It wasn't meant to go this way and yet here we were. Homeless with only a change of clothes and a toothbrush each. Martin wouldn't even let me take the kids' beds. I couldn't believe he was doing this to us.

After a few days I came to the realization how Martin refusing to leave was actually a blessing in disguise. I would set up our own new home the way I wanted to. This way I got to decide what happened next. A bit like those choose-your-own-adventure books I used to read as a kid.

But this optimism was hard to hold on to over the next few months as Martin seemed intent on making my life as difficult as possible. He was angry. He wasn't going to let me just start again. He was intent on making me pay for leaving him.

It was mid-December when I received an unexpected letter. I read the word "lawyers" and completely froze. As I opened the envelope, hands trembling, I knew it was going to take all the emotional strength I could muster not to break down in tears on the front lawn. I couldn't wait to get inside, I had to read it now. I had to know what I was facing.

As I read the first line, I could feel my body reacting. My heart started beating faster and I felt that wave of panic I was so used to by now—like being dumped by the surf and not knowing if I would make it to the surface. "My client is seeking fifty-fifty care of the children…" I didn't have to read any further to know I wasn't about to let that happen. It was my job to protect the kids from the abuse they had already suffered. I wasn't going to subject them to further abuse. We had left because I feared his behavior and I could see it escalating. I wasn't about to let him have them alone where I couldn't be there to protect them. Not without a fight. From an outsider's point of view, it was just a bitter separation and dispute between parents, but I knew there was more to it. I knew I wasn't crazy like he'd made me out to be. No matter what it took, I was going to take control of my life again and I was damn sure going to do whatever it took to keep my kids safe.

The next few months were spent speaking to an array of lawyers about my situation and as much as I hated it I came to the realization I would need to facilitate some kind of relationship between the children and Martin or I could suffer the consequences of Family Law Court. I had heard stories from many friends and the outcome had been devastating to the mother and children. I had to maintain some control of the situation to protect the children and the only way to do that was to stay out of Family Law Court. I would have to manage this myself.

Some intense self-care and personal development followed, and I began working on myself and being okay with it just being me and the kids. I was the happiest I'd ever been. This wasn't how I thought life would turn out, but I was happy. I was free. Free to be me, whoever that was! It took some time to figure that out but the more I searched the happier I became. I started doing things I wanted to do purely because they brought me joy. It felt good to do what made me happy with no restrictions and I didn't need to ask permission or feel guilty for spending time alone to recharge.

Life was good, but as much as I enjoyed the alone time when the kids were with their father, I found myself at home alone worrying about them and I needed a distraction. I started spending some of my "me" time browsing an internet dating site. I had no expectations other than to chat and have a bit of fun. I wasn't even sure if I was ready to physically meet another man and I was fully aware a woman with three children in tow could be perceived as having too much "baggage," so I felt safe. I chatted to a few men before coming across the profile of a man called Michael. His profile said *Looking for someone to call home.* Michael and I began chatting online and for the first time in twelve months since the separation with Martin, I had a longing for companionship. I wasn't ready to give up on my fairytale dream, so I thought "what the hell" and agreed to meet Michael.

We met at a local coffee shop (safe I thought) and I had my preschooler and toddler with me so I could make a quick escape if I needed to. I had a last-minute attack of nerves and almost didn't go. I made excuses about not being able to make it (kids are great for that) and Michael sounded disappointed. Something inside of me told me to go, even as my nerves were telling me not to. "What's the worst that could happen?" I thought to myself. If we don't get along it will be awkward for half an hour and then I can make excuses to leave and I never have to see or talk to him again. So I went. When I walked into the coffee shop my heart literally skipped a beat as I saw him sitting at the back of the cafe.

That was three years ago, and we haven't spent a day apart since. Today we are living in our dream suburb in a beautiful four-bedroom house with my three kids and our own baby who is the glue that has stuck us all together. Life is better than I ever imagined it could be and I have finally found my happily ever after.

Did I mention he proposed to me after I gave birth to our daughter? Yep, he's pretty amazing! He is the man I've been waiting for all my life and I would never have found him if I hadn't weathered the storm that came first. Without the rain there would be no rainbow.

ABOUT THE AUTHOR

LOUISE FELTHAM

Louise (Lou) Feltham is a professional speaker, business coach, and entrepreneur from Brisbane, Australia. During her corporate career, Louise successfully navigated the male-dominated industry of property management, rising to a senior position.

Louise has always had ambitious career goals but knew there was more to life than the corporate rat-race. When she became a single mother, she decided to make her dreams a reality. She started her own online business so she could achieve her career goals while also being present for her children.

Four years later, as a mother of four, Louise is successfully running her online business while also launching the Miracle Mums Movement, a service to support and empower women to rise from domestic violence and mental illness.

Invitation from the Author

If you are ready to take control of your life and start creating one of happiness, growth, and fulfillment then #jointhemovement #miraclemumsmovement

www.miraclemumsmovement.com

Business Name: Miracle Mums Movement

Website: www.miraclemumsmovement.com

Facebook URL: https://www.facebook.com/miraclemumsmovement

Email: lou@miraclemumsmovement.com

"You are designed to be whole and complete; to test the waters and reach for the unknown."

Micheline Edwards

Have you ever stopped to look at a patch of moss? The velveteen speckling of lush emerald ground appears to be a single plant. Each parcel, however, contains hundreds or even thousands of individual plants that make up this whole beautiful space.

Individually, each miniscule plant is fragile, maybe even insignificant, but as an interwoven and densely placed group they become strong, vibrant, and resilient enough to withstand foot traffic and whatever else life offers.

Growing up in the seventies, I was labeled part of "The Me Generation." In our house, looking out for number one was not only unacceptable behavior but met with swift repercussions. My mother was a strong advocate of family, togetherness, and image. There was no me, you, or self, only *us*. She enforced this so much that our individual selves were often lost in the unit. This unit was full of love and strong. It did not take me long as a budding adolescent to discover the fragile nature of myself within the unbreakable force of our family. I began to nurture, even fine-tune a strong ability to be like moss—small, but part of something bigger and resilient. I learned to tuck away anything that did not work for me and rise with what was dealt. This did not mean I was built of stone. I became wonderfully adaptable, not always willingly, but capable.

It was also during this time, when I became keenly aware that things in our household were not entirely mainstream. Then again, it was the 1970s—what was normal? I learned much later in adulthood my mother had undiagnosed phycological issues from childhood traumas. This left her with a vivid imagination for coping and me with a quirky and peculiar childhood. All of this became the root of many conflicting messages sent to me about life. My mother created a safe, magical, and loving space for us, one full of art, fairy tales, and partial truths. Mama's eccentric and childlike existence (in my young mind) did not prepare us for the real world.

I began realizing around the age of thirteen how everything in life has a flip side or a deeper structure.

My mother passionately believed and reminded us almost daily that we lived in a culturally inept neighborhood. Because of her belief, Mama did offer us a lively helping of social skills that made me realize there might be more to life than what I was experiencing. So began the infrastructure within me to protect who and what was important to me personally. I had already mastered superb personal survival skills. The age of preserving my inner self had begun. I found a way to survive, to drag everything and everyone else along behind me; to thrive and usually look good doing it. Most people who know me say I am a strong woman. I often resent this because I am exceptionally good at hiding my inner journey.

My childhood summers were spent largely running amok outside in the woods or fields all day. We would create elaborate imaginative adventures, often based on favorite books, going out at dawn to play on the wet grass, drinking from garden hoses, and returning after dark. Our routine of freedom and exploration was only trumped by our need to eat or cool off. Along with the neighborhood kids, I would go from house to house swiping popsicles, scrounging from gardens, and begging whichever mother was around for snacks or the use of a sprinkler. The world was good.

The outdoors is still my happy place. A place of mindful sorting out of life. It is where I am currently writing this, with the breeze sounding like the ocean waves and leaves blowing onto my hammock. Outside in nature everything seems to complement or enhance something else in a seamless harmony of peace.

I remember when fall came, I dreaded being confined inside school all day. The aroma of paper, gum erasers, tempera paint, and books. The sounds of agitated kids tapping, bells ringing, and the sights from the classroom window calling me seemed so conflicting. The only thing that seemed to pull everything together were the books. Books were a big deal in our home. Raised largely without a television, books were the connecting dots to nature, art, life, and adventures! The books were a gateway to endless imagination and becoming a part of whatever, you desired. They were always a part of discovering the world beyond rural mid-America.

The books were so important that as a kid I recall this being something of pride but also embarrassment.

My mother was chummy with the school librarian, which established a familiar and comforting rapport but also detracted from the typical library hour most kids experienced. My mother would also live for our scholastic book orders to arrive soon after the school year began. Many kids never ordered, some usually got a book or two. My friends usually got posters or received a tacky kid's "magazine" with an "explosive" title. If you were raised in the US during the 1970s, then you know the one. Not me, nope! I got stacks of books usually consisting of six to eight books an order.

They were sometimes paid for with an awkward and heavy envelope of spare change. This like everything else in my childhood was confusing. It was both something I looked forward to as they were our home entertainment in the evening, but was also embarrassing, especially because posters and the explosive magazines most kids got, never graced my stack. The bulging, loud, change-filled envelope of course screamed that maybe we should not have ordered so many.

What my mother did order were classics. She stocked our minds with a huge array of both established and what would be forthcoming classics. Caldecott, Newberry, and more were the "wallpaper" in my bedroom growing up. Books filled the immense library shelves that lined my not-so-private library turned bedroom. On high shelves behind my bed were my mother's treasured classics. There were first editions and multitudes of classic books we were not allowed to touch or even smell without permission. Honestly, none of us cared. To me they were forbidden fruit and they could stay that way. The whole thing was yet another weird contradiction in life.

As I got a bit older and began high school my mother, who would never follow up on our homework (another whole book in itself), would begin to recommend or highly encourage that I read some of those "top shelf" books. Honestly, my favorites were her cookbooks, which I had secretly been reading and sneaking back onto the shelves for years.

My mother had a set of first edition Dickens. As a preteen, I honestly did not understand or even care to understand the importance of just how lovely these books and a few others she had really were. At the time they just seemed like a huge diversion or script for life my mother was unable to evolve past.

One evening my mother brought out her precious set of first edition works by Dickens. As with so many things in my life, I was oddly excited but also dreading where I knew this was going.

My mother quoted a line from *A Tale of Two Cities*, which is a love story set during the French revolution. The line she quoted was too cliché for me at the time:

> *"It was the best of times, it was the worst of times, it was the age of wisdom, it was the age of foolishness, it was epoch of belief, it was epic of incredulity, it was the season of Light"*

My mother then handed me a book with the assumption I would read it and left me to do just that. Over the next few years both at my mother's encouragement and because of a few industrious English instructors, I finished most of my mother's treasured Dickens classics.

• • •

Wisdom takes many forms throughout our lives. As children, wisdom seems to be the ability to "wow" other kids with something incredulous and cool, such as a new way to make a cat's cradle, learning to ride a bike, or how to swim. I never learned to do the latter as my mother was also very overprotective and controlling. Her ability to love us beyond belief, combined with her unconscious talent to terrorize us with fear about anything she herself was uncomfortable doing, was uncanny.

As I ventured into my high school years, knowledge began to be all-consuming. It now took the form of driving, knowing what fashions to wear or not wear, who was dating, and of course academics.

As mentioned before, everything done in our family that was not created, instigated, or approved by my mother for the betterment of the family unit was generally met with opposition. Being a teen was both glorious and frustrating in our household. Freedom met my mother's sense of control. Most of us fight this battle as we strive to establish our individual identities and begin to spread our wings to leave the nest.

The summers between my school years came and went, filled with dating, drive-in movies, barbeques with friends, county fairs, and all the things Midwest teenagers do. I continued forward with the mindset that it was indeed the best of times and sometimes what I believed to be the worst of times, but there was always light, and there was always wisdom.

Through my mother's love of knowledge and her need to create a persona of elitism, we were encouraged to act and behave a certain way—to be proper. We were also given no direction beyond table manners and learning to say, "Yes Ma'am." If my mother had been allowed, we probably would have been permanently detained in her imaginary world. Of course, this didn't happen, much to my mother's frustration.

In high school I managed to achieve decent grades and a few choice scholarships. which My road to the future was well-paved despite obstacles. My dream was to study obstetrics, which will soon seem perhaps humorous. Life is always full of crashes courses.

My senior year arrived, and I graduated in late December. In January I enrolled in the local university to get a jump start on my freshman year in college. The battle to study in our home was always quite traumatic. I began to spend more and more time at friends' homes just to complete homework. My detachment from the unit was beginning.

At one point, I vividly remember making a decision that would forever change my future. I did not consciously make this choice knowing it would be as impactful as it was, but I was a young female with a boyfriend. I became pregnant.

I found this out as the school year closed. My thoughts became like a roller coaster going from college to how to handle this situation.

One thing my mother had taught us was to value life. There were a lot of other misguided messages and confusion growing up, but in our home, children were treasures. I knew I was now to become first and foremost a mother. This also established a deep mindfulness of not only how I would do this but also how would I continue my education (alternative schools and the age of teen mother support groups had not quite reached us yet in the 1980s).

How would this affect the image of our family my mother struggled so hard to maintain? Deep down I knew.

I was too young to have a child. As a matter of fact, I was reminded of this by friends, family, school personnel, and society in general. I engaged survival mode. After all, what was done, was done.

Even at this young age, I was no stranger to not only thinking outside of the box but often rebuilding the whole box if necessary, to move forward. I wanted to be a mother someday. To me, reversing the order of things simply meant taking a few embarrassing hits and figuring out a way to continue academics amidst adversity.

The day I told my mother was a warm early summer afternoon. I purposely took her to a local ice-cream shoppe we often frequented. The smell of sugar and milk lingered in the air as we took our usual seats by a window next to a potted plant that my mother had obviously coveted for some time. I purposely took her here because in my eighteen-year-old mind she would not break rank and lose her composure in the ice-cream shoppe. I told her. She sat there for what seemed to be an eternity. I finally muttered something to the effect of knowing this was not "really good timing." My mother sat there a bit longer then spoke. I remember her words vividly, for they reminded me of her Dickens quote from years ago.

> *"It is never really a perfect time to have a child. If we all waited for perfection, there would be no beautiful babies."*

That was it? That was my lecture. That was all she said. We finished our ice-cream.

I went to the car and waited while she walked away to make a quick stop for something.

Later that evening she presented me with three tiny onesies as my father congratulated me. No lectures, no yelling, no life lessons, no predictions of doom, just the message to move forward with what I had and to celebrate where I was.

• • •

Over the next years I did just that. I added an amazing and supportive husband of nearly thirty-five years, five beautiful children, and thirteen grandchildren (so far). I managed to successfully educate myself, my children, and raise my family while incorporating entrepreneurship of several businesses into life.

It is interesting how our weakest moments often become our greatest strengths. I became the owner of a thriving private obstetrical consulting practice. I have been privileged to spent countless hours working with women and welcoming new life into the world. I found a niche caring for and guiding women and young families to be their best while balancing life and family. My mission is to make sure every woman knows how to hear and trust her instincts in every situation and to do things exactly the way she envisioned.

There is never a perfect time to achieve your dreams, have a child, or start a business.

All we have is time, right up until we do not. Waiting to embark on life's next adventure is not an option I ever entertain.

We are always living in a contradictory setting that beautifully illustrates Dickens' words, *"It is the best of times; it is the worst of times."*

If you surround yourself with a supportive community, know who you are, what you want, and equip yourself with knowledge and desire, then there is always a light.

As I write this, I think back to being told I was not old enough to have a baby as a teen. I was told my life would be ruined, that I would likely fail as a parent and as a woman. I remember the hurt I felt as I was looked upon with disgrace and pity even by those, I felt were my community of cheerleaders. Even the hospital staff treated me as a failure before I even began.

If I had allowed all this to sink in, I might have never begun.

I now realize how other people's perceptions of my abilities were skewed according to their own plot in life. I was led to place too much credibility in society's white picket fence illusion.

When I started my adult life and began parenthood, I was told by society I was too young. With my second I was told I did not know what I was getting into. With my third and fourth I was told I must not know "what caused this." They were too close, and everyone was worried about me.

The truth, however, is others were not as concerned about what I was doing as much as how it would affect them if I failed.

By the time my fifth baby arrived, an interesting turn of events also occurred. My friends and family still largely believed I did not know what caused pregnancy. I was becoming an older and more experienced mom. The condescending hospital staff in a sense ignored me other than to give me a sterilization lecture. Of course, the nurse who rudely did this was not aware I was a professional who counseled and taught reproductive health. I listened, smiled, and did my thing.

As my mother wisely told me, in life if we wait for the perfect moment to begin our lives, to achieve our dreams, to move forward with our visions, then we will forever be waiting.

I never realized it was through my mother's quirky, eccentric, and often embarrassing ways that frequently hurled me into so many conflicting and difficult situations that what she had actually given me was a crash course in resiliency, tenacity, and the vast imagination to dream big even when the world might be telling me "no."

You are not too young, too old, or not enough. You are wonderfully and gloriously made to do exactly what your heart desires—you just need to believe and do it!

You are not a single thought, dream, or experience. Like moss, you are built of many tiny facets that create a strong, resilient structure.

Setbacks happen. Life and society often seem to be steering your dreams. Draw upon all your wisdom, believe in yourself, grab hold of your own steering wheel and you will rise for tomorrow. A favorite quote of mine is by Erin Hanson:

> *"There is a freedom waiting for you, on the breezes of the sky. And you ask, 'What if I fall?' Oh, but my darling, what if you fly?"*

I have always been blessed with knowing what I wanted to do in life. I wanted a family and to work with women to achieve their dreams. I have largely been surrounded by magical mentors, but often, like my mother, their presence was not obvious at the time. Messages frequently became long voyages. If you desire clarity and mentorship to accomplish your dreams, I would love to assist you in defining your Life Code of Rights and establishing your own *Gated Community*.

ABOUT THE AUTHOR

MICHELINE EDWARDS

Micheline Edwards is a bestselling author and Certified Health and Life Coach who has been changing the lives of women for more than twenty-five years. She is the founder and creator of *Your Life Code of Rights* and *Gated Communities*, coaching platforms based on her experience as a labor and delivery provider that are designed for encouraging positive life engagement.

She enjoys public speaking, conducting group seminars, and holding retreats for women. Micheline is a Certified Bars Facilitator and Reiki Master. She has been a Midwife,

Lactation Counselor, Doula (a charter member of DONA), and a Parent/Family Educator who has guided hundreds of women through some of their most intimate transitions in life.

Micheline's blog, *Five Children and a Farm*, touches on the spiritual side of life as well as the events of raising a large family while being a busy female entrepreneur. Her passion for life leads her to embrace every moment with celebration and she guides her clients to do the same. She is blessed to be married for nearly thirty-five years to her childhood sweetheart. Micheline and her husband Doyle have five successful, beautiful grown children who were home educated, as well as an ever-growing nest of grandchildren.

Invitation from the Author

Visit my website for an exclusive gift to begin an amazing life!

www.Michelineedwards.com/sherises4tomorrow

Business Name: Micheline Edwards Transformational Coaching

Website: www.michelineedwards.com

Facebook URL:
https://www.facebook.com/MichelineTransformationalCoach

Email: Pinerockfarms@hotmail.com

"Hope, vision, and success have a way of slipping into your life when you learn to love that person in the mirror."

Kathy Denise Hicks

Asleep and comfortable in my warm twin bed, I was awakened by the blinding overhead light. My five-year-old brain couldn't make sense of what was happening. Slowly I rose from bed and my mom handed me a laundry basket and told me to pack some things and that we were moving. My life would never be the same.

You see, unbeknownst to me, mom and dad had been having problems for a while. They were young when they married. My dad liked to have a drink or two. My mom was a very headstrong woman, who had a vision for her life and the life of her children. So, she decided to take my brother and I and create a new way of life.

We moved from place to place, every two years. I was the "new kid" everywhere we went. The shyness and my inclination to live inside my head grew as I struggled to make friends. My mom worked hard as a nurse to provide for us, but money was tight. I remember being teased for wearing secondhand clothes. An intense drive began to grow within my spirit. I knew I would someday show others this poorly dressed, mis-matched girl was not the "real me." Someday I would show everyone who I really was. Until then, I kept to myself, helping my mom as best as I could. I began cooking dinner for her. With no friends, I had lots of time to spend on my own, teaching myself piano and singing songs I made up.

By the time I reached thirteen, I decided I wanted to get to know my father. I had kept in touch with him and had summers with him through the years. I decided to move out of my mom's house and in with him. I was still that same shy, insecure girl, but I was excited to get a new start. I started putting roots down and made a few friends. For six years I lived with my dad. When it came time to decide what direction to go in college, my dad's advice was to pick something like secretarial school or typing. I felt insulted he didn't see me as something more than a secretary. The drive I had felt when teased as a child kicked in and I was determined to become more and prove to my dad I had more ambition than he gave me credit for.

My college years began with me moving out on my own. I had a full-time job, and I began taking calculus during my lunch hour. It was so exciting and new to me. I loved the challenge of the schoolwork. After trying out four majors, I ended up settling for civil engineering.

During these college years, I began discovering more about myself. I was daring and loved exploring new things. I took flying lessons for several months and almost took my first solo flight. I chose to focus on school, so I ended my flying interests. I then traveled across the country on my own and stopped at many amazing places. My confidence grew as I took the classes required of me and I continued to thrive. I became the president of the civil engineering honor society and created many fun and exciting activities for the club. I even hosted a national conference for ten other colleges with great success. Slivers of the "real" me began to shine through, as I changed through these experiences.

My final semester of college brought several huge, amazing life changes for me. First, I was introduced to my future husband on a blind date. Secondly, I finished my college career in London, participating in a study abroad program. This experience proved to be a game-changer for my life and brought with its incredible opportunities for personal growth. Once completed, I continued traveling in Europe for several months, alone for most of the time. I was exhausted from traveling and keeping my guard up. Then the time finally came for me to go home. I was excited to see my boyfriend back at home and start my engineering career at the job I had attained before my trip. Little did I know what was in store for me when I got home.

• • •

My homecoming was amazing, and I was so excited to be in the US again. It was wonderful to be able to rest fully and not worry about thieves and pickpockets. My boyfriend and I began the journey to pick up my things from college. The plan was to stop shortly for dinner at my cousin's place and continue for several hours to pack my personal items being stored by my college roommates during my trip. The dinner was to be a celebratory dinner for both my graduation from college and getting home from my extensive trip, not to mention the first game of that year's Major League Baseball World Series. My cousin's place was on the second story of a typical horse barn. The stairs leading up to the loft apartment were wooden and rickety. My host had gone to great lengths to prepare this feast.

As we were sitting down to dinner and getting ready to enjoy our first bite, "it" happened. I say "it" because at that moment, I didn't know if it was an explosion from an air attack, or gas tank, or perhaps a car. During the next ten seconds, "it" became clear what was happening. I glanced at my dinner companions, and we each had anxious, questioning looks on our faces. Movement of the whole floor began, side-to-side. I noticed a hanging crystal on the window and fully expected either the crystal or the window would shatter.

My heart was beating out of my chest and my mind was racing with panicked thoughts such as, "Am I going to get out of this? Is someone going to find us buried in this barn?" And the question many probably ask on their death beds, "Is this it?"

The shaking stopped, we gathered our courage, and bounded down the stairs. Once outside, we found a field away from fallen structures and stopped to collect ourselves and try to process what had happened.

My mind rejoiced we had survived this nightmare of a natural disaster. What I didn't know was how my personal nightmare was just beginning.

All was well, or so I thought, until a recurring nightmare began haunting me, night after night. It was always the same realistic dream. The earthquake would start, the beams in the living room would dislodge and fall, and my roof would open up to show the sky. The dreams became worse, and finally I decided if I didn't sleep, I wouldn't dream.

My spirit beaten and fatigued; life became too hard. Part of me wanted to end this nightmare of a life. But the drive that had been with me since my childhood compelled me to find help and guidance during this difficult time. I allowed a counselor to speak truth and life to me, and she guided me to a group program. From this I began to grow and change.

I developed habits like prayer and meditation. The "real" me slowly began to emerge again. At first, I despised the person in the mirror. So many wrong turns, mistakes, memories, and regrets. As time went on, my self-loathing turned into acceptance and compassion. These changes were slow, but steady. Little did I know what was on the next horizon of my life—something I didn't plan on, that is for sure.

That time of discovery was put on hold for a bit. Within several years, I married the man of my dreams. He was stable and such a wonderful person. We had three children with a set of twins in the mix. The twins were a bit of work, for sure, and quite taxing on my body and mind. When they were babies, I returned to my engineering job. By that time, I was a registered engineer, working part time and trying to juggle life as a professional woman with three children and a husband.

After a short time, I noticed my memory and ability to perform easy calculations beginning to slip here and there. I didn't think much of it until I noticed my hands and feet shaking profusely. I couldn't stop the shaking. I also noticed I was losing a lot of weight. This actually excited me at first, until I needed a whole new wardrobe. Medical tests confirmed I had developed Grave's Disease, which was hereditary and probably triggered by stress. At first, I was able to hide my condition at work, checking and double-checking calculations and drafting I had done on the computer. Eventually, my supervisor began noticing inconsistencies and mistakes. Clients began requesting I not work on their projects.

Finally, one day in May, I was fired and given one hour to pack my things and go home. Devastated, embarrassed, and emotionally bankrupt, I went home. I remember sitting in my room, trying to figure out what I was going to tell my husband. I broke the news to him, and we began to figure out a plan of how we would survive financially, as we had just bought a house. Luckily, I had documented my illness and cognitive issues. I went on disability for a year and towards the end of the year and my husband found a new job to replace my income.

• • •

The next ten years were spent at home with my kids. I brought them home from public school and chose to homeschool them. It was probably the hardest part of my life but also the most rewarding. I ended up having two more children, bringing the final count to five—four boys and one girl. We enjoyed homeschooling, but eventually they begged to go back to school. As my youngest needed educational support I couldn't provide, I enrolled her in school. It felt like it was time to go back to work.

Because my Graves' Disease had resolved itself through diet, exercise, and prayer, I figured I would give engineering a try again. I started part-time and found all the computer programs had changed so much I practically had to start over. I wanted to quit every day, but the drive that had been with me through every challenge and gotten me through would not let me give up. I studied videos to help me relearn the computer programs. I studied at night to re-learn the design standards and regulations for various jurisdictions. As time progressed, I enrolled in a week-long computer class, which filled in the ten-year gaps I had in my computer skills and knowledge.

I began to experience amazing progress and was actually challenged by developing my abilities in design and producing construction drawings. I was asked to apply my skills in construction plans and reports. I felt I had really broken through a barrier that had previously left me without confidence in my ability as an engineer. Feelings of accomplishment and pride really began to shine through. More than that, a feeling of self-worth and being worthy of success. I began to not only know who I really was, but also to genuinely like the person in the mirror.

Although I was truly enjoying engineering, I knew something was missing. I didn't think I was put on the earth to sit in front of a computer screen. I felt I was meant for more. That sense of drive, which had been with me all those years, pushed me into another career. Something more aligned with the "real me" I had been searching for.

• • •

Nutrition and exercise have been important throughout my whole life. I have always been active in sports in school. As a teen, I remember being teased at what I included in my diet. While others around me were eating junk food, I loved salads and veggies. Don't get me wrong, I love a good burger and fries now and then, but this healthy way of eating has always been a focus in my life. I now realize part of why I paid attention to my diet was my dad's extensive family history of heart disease. About ten years ago, my father passed away from a massive heart attack. After that, I made exercise and nutrition even more important part of my life.

I made working out a part of my everyday routine, even when my kids were young. This habit followed me when I went back to work. I would participate in bootcamps at 5:30 am just to get my workouts in, and still have time to pick my kids up from school every day, which was another of my priorities. I eventually began playing with the idea of becoming a personal trainer. I interviewed trainers and began looking at programs I could fit into my busy lifestyle. I was still working as an engineer, trying to get my remaining two kids through school, keep my house running, and all the while attempt to remain healthy.

The decision was made, and I enrolled in an online program. The goal was to become certified as both a personal trainer and a corrective exercise specialist. My little "drive" had gone into "overdrive," but I was determined to complete both courses and pass the difficult exams. I spent many nights studying the course material between helping my kids with their homework and projects and working at my engineering job during the day.

Success! I passed my personal trainer exam. My next goal was to complete and pass my corrective exercise specialist exam. One day after studying into the early morning, a thought passed through my mind. Why? Why do I start something so difficult that I will knock myself out and almost sacrifice my relationships and my health? Why do I jump from goal to goal? I am never satisfied but always wanting something new and different. I had a huge epiphany after I pondered this question for some time. Yes, I had drive and ambition. But it finally came to me how I had been always trying to get my father's approval. In every endeavor I had attempted over the years, I just wanted him to be proud. I realized I needed to let go of my imagination or story of what I believed he thought about me. Just let it go. He was gone, and I needed to drive my own ship and not allow someone or something else "drive" me anymore.

A huge relief was lifted from my spirit and I felt free to really pursue my dreams and goals. Any thought of either parent being disappointed left me, as well as all disappointment I had in myself. I finally uncovered the rest of "me" and truly loved the person in the mirror. I could now begin to let who I was and who I was becoming shine forth in the world. I could share the gifts, talents, and skills I already had, with the world. If I chose, I could develop more skills and use them as a part of the world I was creating.

This was a huge breakthrough for me. I was previously driven for the wrong reasons. It is so much easier to run forward when you're not looking back. I passed my corrective exercise specialist exam, which, by the way, felt more difficult than my three-day engineering registration exam. I decided to pursue certifications in several other exercise modalities, all of which, would help me facilitate positive change in my clients' lives. Things were rolling along splendidly until March 2020, which brought yet another crazy, life-altering event.

Similar to what it felt like when I lost my engineering job more than ten years prior, one morning I was asked to pack up my computer and take it home. Several people at work were sick and a new, very serious virus was spreading in our area. My workplace took swift action and sent everyone home. It took quite a while to acclimate to my new working environment. You see, I was rarely ever home at this point in my life. I worked full time, taught seven exercise classes a week, had several personal training clients, and drove my teenagers from activity to activity. Several days later, the world shut down, including the gyms and my daughter's school.

My life was turned upside down. I was just getting traction in my training business. I developed a mild depression, and the freeze response was invoked in my world. I didn't know what to do, so I did what everyone else did during this time and the refrigerator became my best friend. My snack and comforter of choice was Kit Kat, a favorite candy bar. This went on for some time, probably about a month.

Then one day I awoke feeling entirely fed up with my status quo and decided to change my daily routine. I began posting on social media that I was offering free exercise classes. Several friends began to join me, but I knew I needed help starting an online business. I ended up joining a coaching mastermind program to help me achieve my goals. This was the first major investment I had made in myself. I was finally ready to make my dreams of developing a health and fitness business a reality.

Blueprint Fitness became real. I had been developing my website, phone app, logo, and brand for the past year, not knowing how it would come into play. Since April 2020, all the pieces have begun to fall into place. I recently developed a six-week course called Fit Life Blueprint, to help women forty and older develop daily habits to alleviate pain, increase range of motion, and attain and maintain their ideal weight. Fit Life Blueprint utilizes mindset, exercise, and nutrition to help women make small shifts in their lifestyle resulting in large changes in their health. I incorporate my engineering training by being very attentive to detail in movement and form, focusing on the client to ensure injuries do not occur. It has been inspiring to see my clients enjoy a level of fitness and health they previously had trouble achieving.

The struggles and trials that I have been through, have helped form the character and self-belief that I now possess. I know there is so much more to my story and I am excited to see what the next adventure will be. As my business grows, many more opportunities to change lives will become available. I look forward to the future with anticipation and expectancy, now able to incorporate my passion in health and fitness to inspire those around me to make healthy life choices.

ABOUT THE AUTHOR

KATHY DENISE HICKS

Kathy Denise Hicks is an ex-Civil Engineer turned certified Personal Trainer, Corrective Exercise Specialist, and Yamuna (Body Rolling) Instructor.

She empowers people to incorporate habits that alleviate joint and muscular pain, increase energy, and help them attain their ideal weight. Kathy's mantra "No Pain, More Gain" is truly exemplified through her coaching techniques and expertise. Her Fit Life Blueprint course has helped many women create their dream bodies.

She lives in northern California with her husband of thirty years with their five grown children. You will catch her teaching and developing exercise classes or writing while gazing at the beauty of neighboring vineyards.

Invitation from the Author

Visit my website for a FREE virtual fitness training session to help you activate a healthier body and mind:

www.blueprintfitness.net

Business Name: Blueprint Fitness

Website: https://blueprintfitness.net/

Facebook URL: https://www.facebook.com/coach.khicks

Email: kathy@blueprintfitness.net

"The most important kind of freedom is to be who you really are. Our task must be to free ourselves as human beings so we can speak our truth and follow our own path. And that is where our greatness lies."

Pia Prana Muggerud

I have just finished my studies in Edinburgh, Scotland, and I am arriving back to my home in Norway. Having just finished five years of studying, I am finally free to step out in the world. The image still clear in my mind is one of excitement and wonder to start this next important chapter in my life. However, as I am contemplating this new chapter, I am feeling a heaviness inside. My head is slightly bowed, and I keep asking myself why am I feeling so empty?

This question leaves me baffled. I have been working so hard over the last five years, with the aim of making something of myself. I have done all the right things society tells me to do—I have worked hard in school and focused on getting good grades in high school. I secured a place at a prestigious university in Scotland. I finally completed my degree and was subsequently invited back for an additional year, which was paid for by a grant for only the best students. As I sit contemplating all my achievements thus far, there is a sinking feeling inside that I don't want any of this. I never did.

This realization comes as a shock to me, I wonder to myself how I have not come to this realization before now. I have been heading in one direction all my life until this moment. I have ticked all the required boxes, and now I am sitting here questioning the entire script of my life. It seems I have not been the author of my own script. A voice inside me is screaming, "Then who the hell is the author?" Some clarity begins to emerge through my inner fog. I start getting a clearer image of how I ended up in this moment—confused, angry, and not wanting the life I have so meticulously built for myself. How many times was I told to *be a "good girl?" Do as you're told. Don't talk back. Wait your turn. Don't make trouble. Smile and look happy. Make your parents happy.* Where *are your manners? Just sit and be quiet.* As all these messages come pouring into my consciousness, like the credits at the end of a movie, I see now how these messages have come from so many directions, and I have simply believed them to be true. I have taken them as my scripture, the rules I must live by. I have become the culturally acceptable "*good girl.*" I had learned to please others at the expense of myself. Being a *good girl* means I have been suppressing a lot.

As I sit there allowing the movie credits of my life to complete their download, I am struck by more than just a feeling of inner discontent. There is another, new feeling inside. As I listen more closely, I realize there is a sense of relief bubbling inside. Although the sense of relief is very faint, it gives rise for me to do something totally out of character. The *good girl* in me is screaming for me to press the pause button on this new plan. Yet there is a stronger, more alive part inside growing bigger every moment. And this is the voice of the rebel, the one who wants to live with more passion, with more aliveness, with truth and with adventure. All this, coupled with the crumbled dream of a relationship with a man I have known and loved since childhood, I hear a firm voice inside: "What have you got to lose?" That is the voice that wins, and I step onto a plane. I fly eighteen hours, crossing countries and continents, ending up in Hong Kong. This move is definitely not part of the boxes to be ticked. However, this move is a step away from where all the rules originate from. I want to go somewhere far way, where I can write my own rules.

• • •

It is a grey November afternoon, and I am sitting on a bus. As I look outside there is nothing familiar, no friendly images that make me feel at home. Instead, I am on a strange road, in a strange country. I have just stepped off a long-haul flight, and it feels inconceivable that only hours earlier I was home in Norway, feeling the fire of my inner rebel and brave girl. Instead, I am now feeling anxious, scared and very lonely.

I have just landed in Hong Kong and I am on my way from the airport to the city. What I am looking at cannot be more different than what I am used to. As I look out the window of the bus, all I can see are grey high-rise buildings. The scene reminds me of a movie set from a war-torn city. Everything is grey and dark. I feel shocked and have a sense of dread about what else I might find here. As I sit there, I contemplate how leaving home to travel to Scotland was an easy move, a piece of cake. I had grown up surrounded by beauty, with stunning nature, clear blue skies, mountains, and fjords. This is a big shock to my system.

What have I done? What am I doing here? Maybe I can just turn around and head back home! As much as I want to run away from this moment, the voice of the *good girl* inside would never allow it. She reminds me I have made my decision and I have to stick to it, no matter how hard it is or how lost I am feeling in this moment. Just before the bus reaches its final destination, I remember back to my childhood and a story we were told about China. If you start digging a hole and you dig deep enough, you will reach China. I giggle to myself thinking back at this silly story. Never in a million years did I ever think I would end up in this part of the world. And I certainly could not dream in this moment that Hong Kong would become my home for twenty-five years.

• • •

I am not arriving on totally cold ground in Hong Kong. I am visiting my dear friend Cathie from university. She is a bubbly, fun, vivacious girl, and through her I am not just invited to the city, but I receive an instant "green light" to join her exciting and fun group of friends. The sense of enthusiasm is bubbling inside as I meet people from all over the world—each one with a more inspiring or unique story to tell. My new friends joke they are living like students, but the difference being they have a salary. I learn early that in this city, people don't just work hard, they also play equally hard. I quickly drop into this mentality, starting with the playing hard.

Being so far away from home, I also get the sense we play by different rules here. This somehow excites me, as I feel I have been living inside a prison of so many rules, but here I feel I can do anything! Each new person I meet has so much to teach me, and through their many often courageous stories, my eyes open to a new world, multicolored and multifaceted. I thrive in this new-found courage, where I learn to scuba dive, where I go solo backpacking to tropical countries like Thailand and Indonesia. It feels like life can't get any better!

I am in love with Hong Kong, and although I have only been planning to stay a few months, I soon start to think about what I might be able to do in this vibrant city. University, however, has not prepared me for the requirements and challenges of working in such a fast-paced and international environment. Even as a fresh graduate I am expected to get myself up to speed, and the unspoken expectations are I just have to handle it. I manage to get away with pretending I know what I am doing for a while. But the first job does not last very long. And neither does the second job. By the third job, the pressure is really taking a toll on me. The expectations and the hard work ethic are extremely high. I realize the hard way how I am not even allowed to be sick. As I lie in bed sick and miserable, I receive a call from the office, with a message that my boss does not care if I was in a wheelchair, I better come to work!

I subsequently get fired from this job for no reason. As a *good girl*, I am so used to conforming—don't make waves, don't rock the boat. This means I am used to pretending a lot. So, I don't speak up about how wrong this feels to me right now. Yet in this moment I feel like I have hit rock bottom. My self-image of being good is completely shattered and I cry myself to sleep, all alone. *What is the point? I have done everything that has been expected of me.* I have focused on being a people-pleaser, being the ultimate *good girl*, and it has cost me dearly.

● ● ●

The truth of the matter is I don't enjoy my chosen subject—interior design. I never have. As a teenager my passion showed itself loud and clear - psychology. Even at such an early age I had a deep yearning to understand the human psyche. It is what I needed for myself, for my sanity. I lit up reading books on the subject and got top marks in my psychology elective in high school. Why I didn't study psychology is unclear to me now so many years later. One thing I know for sure is that I would have chosen my subject from a deep place inside that needed to adhere to some unspoken social expectations. Now I am sitting here, baffled, confused, and with a voice inside my head instructing me I must continue this path because that's what I have committed to when I studied. Yet another rule, I think to myself, that I am supposed to obey.

The people-pleaser is also showing up in many other areas of my life. It isn't easy for me to catch it in the moment; the moment where I find myself not listening to what MY truth is. The biggest area of both interest for me as well as pain is that of intimate relationships. Like so many girls and young women, I dream of meeting my Prince Charming. And yet, I am not able to make this area of my life work. I want so desperately to please, to meet men's expectations, so they will not reject me, so they will love me. I find myself smiling when I feel sad, telling men things I think they want to hear rather than being truthful. And of course, most of the time I am not being truthful to myself, as I am so deeply rooted in my *good girl* identity. The most extreme manifestation of this, what I call the curse of the *good girl*, shows up for me in promiscuous behavior. I am living an illusion, and I am convinced that if I sleep with a man, then he will love me. Every time, however, without fail, I wake up to the cold, painful, lonely realization that I am as far away from love as I could possibly be.

• • •

I am hanging out at home one evening when the phone rings. As I pick up the phone, I hear my father's voice and I notice it is slightly more muted than usual. He starts by telling me he had hoped he wouldn't have to make this call. He had hoped my mother would become healthier, but this is not to be. My mother has suffered with depression and anxiety over the years. Due to early childhood trauma, she suffered a type of self-abandonment my father now explains to me has resulted in a type of psychosis that is no longer manageable. As I hang up the phone and begin to plan my flight back to Norway, a cold numbness takes over my insides. I feel afraid. There is a sense of disbelief, yet it also doesn't surprise me that my mother's increasing instability has been kept from me. I am used to us keeping secrets in our family, or rather not being up-front with the truth. I am used to us putting up a façade for the outside world. I get on the flight, my inner *good girl* takes over, and I make myself ready to take on the role of caretaker for the rest of my family.

• • •

When I walk through the door of my parents' home, I am not quite prepared for the shock of seeing my mother. But I want to be helpful, so I put on a brave face, I smile, and put aside my own distraught feelings as I get on with taking care of mum. My being here helps my father to be able to continue going to work as we wait for my mum to be institutionalized. One thing that gives me strength is the fact that I have worked for several years in the same mental institution. I know the place well and I have seen how well they take care of their patients there. This thought gives me some peace of mind and a sense it will be good for my mum to be there.

• • •

One morning when I wake up, my mother missing. It is snowing outside, ice cold, and I have no idea where to start looking for her. The car is still in the garage and she goes nowhere without it. So, I find myself running along the river in front of my parents' house, frantically looking for her. I even look in the ice-cold water for her. After what feels like an eternity for me, I finally find her. As I approach her, it feels like nobody is there. I am flooded with so many feelings—everything from anger and despair to sadness and grief.

It's a few weeks later, I am back in Hong Kong, and mum is receiving the help she needs. I have been feeling pleased about how I was able to support my family around my mother's illness, yet in this moment I feel life is very dark. I cannot seem to shift the heaviness that is building up inside. As the days go by, the heaviness turns into emptiness and I find myself crying inconsolably daily. The empty hole I feel inside feels like a bottomless pit. And all I seem to be able to do is cry.

• • •

Over the course of the next twelve months, I get though my life in a daze. I am engulfed by depression. My mother's illness has been a catalyst to opening the door to my own personal despair. I cannot be seen like this. I cannot let myself even speak to others about my pain. I am so grateful to my flat-mate's kitten, who keeps me company in my darkest moments. No matter how much I want to escape my inner turmoil, I also realize there is nowhere to go with these tears. I must be with them, to feel feelings that have been buried for most of my life. And I must come face to face with the fear that I will become like my mum.

• • •

As the year anniversary of my mother's illness comes closer, my inner strength and determination returns. I have spent the last year mostly on my own, but more importantly, what has kept me going is a wish to carry my life forward without the burdens my mother and those before her have had to carry. This inner fire brings me on a journey, on a search for deeper meaning. I am introduced to personal development, first through books I picked up and then through a friend's introduction to group work. I am devouring anything that can support me to put words to the feelings that are racing inside my body. I become obsessed with looking within and the importance of inner reflection leads me to meditation, to therapy, and slowly back to myself.

• • •

My inner journey leads me to a significant outer journey to India. Through the support of an enlightened master's vision, my darkest moments lead to my greatest breakthroughs. I re-parent my inner child and slowly find the connection between my personal history and that of my family. I am walking the path now I wanted to embrace so many years ago but somehow didn't have the courage—psychology. I dance for no reason. I cry. And I learn and experience, perhaps for the first time, the value of speaking my truth—that I can be loved even when I am not good, or pretty, or have it all together.

• • •

As I delve deeper and deeper into places that have been so hidden to me, I start to recognize an unfamiliar feeling:

love! I am standing in front of a mirror and I can look myself in the eye. I am smiling at the image looking back at me. I have just completed a deep personal process and my eyes are bloodshot and puffy, but I am able to see past that. In this moment, I trust myself and I see my own beauty. I can say yes to my intuition and my inner instincts as truth rather than being the slave of someone else's dogma.

• • •

*"…Thank you India
Thank you terror
Thank you disillusionment
Thank you frailty
Thank you consequence
Thank you thank you silence…"*
(Alanis Morissette – "Thank you")

My travels to India continue every year, always returning to the meditation center that opened up my inner world to me. I am in awe of the strength and resilience I find every time I do my work here, both with meditation and with therapy. It's 2009, and the financial crisis has put a halt to all my work. Everything is cancelled by clients wanting to save money. Despite this fact, I feel strong and trusting, knowing my yearly visit to this place nurtures my soul as nothing else can. In fact, my India trips have become non-negotiable. This time entering the gates something new happens. I see him. I feel myself feeling him. His blue eyes reach me in a way I do not recognize. It takes me two months to dare to come close to him, and when I find myself standing opposite him, I feel my fear and at the same time I jump in. He makes me feel safe, and I feel at home. We are from different worlds. We live continents apart. What comes next might seem foolish to those who are practical, to the uninspired. Pravas and I embark on a love story that is somehow out of our hands. I feel like this moment was always destined to happen. Our love story results in the meeting of two continents in a deepening inner and outer adventure together.

• • •

It is a one year into our relationship. It is still long distance, which keeps both our longing and missing each other alive. We are making the best of being together long distance, but it hasn't been easy for either of us. Having him in my life brings a new strength inside me. I can breathe easier. I feel like whatever life throws at me; I can handle it with Pravas by my side. Pravas has just arrived back in Asia, and we are getting settled into a little flat we have rented together for the summer. Sitting on our little balcony, overlooking lush jungle, I cannot help but feel grateful we are finally spending more time together.

• • •

In the middle of my musings the phone rings. I am not expecting it to be my father on the other end of the line this early in the morning. His solemn voice tells me something is not okay. The next few minutes are a blur, my world is spinning, and somewhere in the distance I can hear a loud scream. It takes me some time to realize it is me who is screaming. I am on the ground. I curl up as tightly as I can, as if by curling up I can disappear from this moment. As a confused Pravas runs into the room, all he can do is hold me.

• • •

My father has just told me my mother has taken her own life. Despite her deep struggles with the pain from her childhood, this shock pierces me to my core. And as we prepare to fly the following day back to Norway, I cannot speak. I feel if I utter any words about it out loud, it will become more real. But it is real. All the painful violent ending to her life is real. As we board the flight, all I can do is sit there and allow the tears to overwhelm me, to grip me in a way nothing has ever gripped me before. And I wonder silently to myself if I will ever recover from this. It is impossible to give this event its appropriate significance here, for it would be a book in itself. How can I fully express how deep this trauma goes? What I can say is that my previous inner work has given me a floor to fall onto.

• • •

It's 2020 as I write this. More than ten years have passed since that impossibly painful day and year. As I think back, I am grateful for so many of the decisions I have made over the years. I decided I didn't want to figure life out on my own and instead reached out for help from coaches and therapists. I am grateful I was brought to meditation and breath work that guides me to a deeper and more intimate relationship with my body and its wisdom. I'm grateful when Pravas walked into my life and I didn't listen to the fearful voice inside whispering "you're gonna get hurt," but instead took a chance on love.

• • •

A therapist many years ago asked me if I could choose, would I choose a different mother and not have the learnings, or choose the same mother and gratefully receive all the wisdom that came with her. As I think back to that question, I remember how easy it was to answer. Of course, I choose my mother.

• • •

It was rarely easy with her, but thanks to her I have grown into a woman who started asking questions early. There have been so many reasons to give up, but thanks to my mum I am resilient, I am courageous, and I am wise. I have lived all over the world, from America to the Middle East and Far East. I have lived a mostly fearless life, or at least jumped in despite the fear.

• • •

It is my soul's mission that helped me eventually, that brought me back to life and into my power. What a beautiful reverberation after so many years, to listen to my inner calling and stop being what society expected. My biggest achievement, and the absolute privilege of my life, is to work with and support people who want to find more authenticity, love, and joy in their lives. And I am convinced if we all focus on these, then we can create a better world.

ABOUT THE AUTHOR

PIA PRANA MUGGERUD

Pia Prana Muggerud is a Holistic Counsellor and Coach, Keynote Speaker, and BioDynamic Breathwork and Trauma Release System® certified Breath Practitioner. She is also a Learning Love teacher and facilitates various women's circles like Awakening of Love and Path of Love.

The loss of self she lived with for many years as a "good girl" got her deeply involved in spiritual and personal growth work over the past twenty years. She draws on a rich background of training and experience in spiritual studies, breath-work, awareness training, and meditation. She is passionate about supporting women to love and put themselves first. She is a re-igniter for women who have abandoned themselves but now want to come out of hiding and claim their rightful place in the world, rising to their authentic greatness.

Pia Prana lives with her husband Pravas between two amazing vibrant cities—Berlin, Germany, and Hong Kong. For the past twenty-five years she has lived on a small tropical island in the South China Sea where she gets to live the best of both worlds—a quiet village life with the city metropolis nearby.

Invitation from the Author

Visit my website for a FREE e-book to discover your irresistible self!

www.co-pia.com

Business Name: Copia Coaching and Training

Website: www.co-pia.com

Facebook URL: https://www.facebook.com/pia.muggerud/

Email: pia@co-pia.com

"Self-care is not a luxury...it is a non-negotiable."

Brooklynn Bradley-LaFleur

I spent a lot of my childhood inside the only hair-salon-bookstore in the world run by my aunt who owned (and still owns) the largest meeting and discussing book club in the world. My mother was a stay-at-home mom my whole life until she earned her real estate license my junior year of high school.

Mom put a lot of effort into trying to convince me to go to school for anything other than hair. She didn't have benefits and had to rely on my father for those and didn't want that for me. So, I went to school to be an English teacher. I didn't make the best grades and would change my schedule each semester because my heart wasn't in it. I loved writing and reading, but being an English teacher wasn't setting my soul on fire, and it showed.

Dad called me one day and said, "Just go apply for cosmetology school, your mom will be fine." So I did, and she was, but only on the condition I stay in a bigger city and not move back to our little town and work for my aunt, which of course is exactly what I had always dreamed of doing.

I bounced around from salon to salon because I wasn't happy. Do you see a pattern here?

Three salons later I called my dad, called my aunt, found a house to rent, and moved back to my sweet little hometown of Historic Jefferson, Texas.

After five long years I was finally doing what I had always wanted to do. If you are lucky enough to know what sets your soul on fire, don't waste your time doing something else.

It was a beautiful day in June 2012. I was walking up the front steps of the quaint little red building that used to be a Texaco oil warehouse and was overcome with a flood of emotions. This is what I had dreamed of. Working alongside my Aunt Kathy at the only hair salon/bookstore in the world, Beauty and the Book, and helping grow her already larger-than-life book club, The Pulpwood Queens.

Over the next few months, I tried to learn as much as I could from her. I was basically fresh out of cosmetology school and never had anyone to mentor me at the other salons I worked in, so I was thankful to have the downtime to watch her work and listen to her explain her methods.

When you are trying to build a clientele there is a lot of downtime. It is also hard to make yourself come to work when you know all you are going to do is sit there, but you have to fill the void with something to help grow your business. I decided to study her method of foiling, how she cut and styled hair, and asked every question I could think of.

It takes time to build a clientele no matter what business you are in. Be patient.

Less than a year after I began my dream job and a few months after getting engaged, I walked in the front door of the salon early on a Tuesday morning to what would be the biggest turning point in my career.

Aunt Kathy was sitting at her desk, typing away as usual, when she looked up at me and said, "I have something to tell you. You will not believe it." She was right. My stomach turned with anticipation for what I knew was going to be terrible news.

She and her husband of twenty-five years were splitting up and I was faced with a choice I was not prepared to make—either purchase her business and take over her building lease by Friday or go find a new job.

Buy her business? I was just a baby hairdresser! I had no money, a very small clientele, home expenses, and I had only begun to really learn a thing or two. Plus, I couldn't even imagine not working with her. We had so much fun together.

Panic set in as my stomach started churning. What was I going to do? I felt like everything was crashing down around me, but I had to snap out of it because I was not the one getting divorced after twenty-five years of marriage.

It was time to sink or swim.

With shaky hands, panic in my voice, and severe anxiety about my future, I called my dad, who is my go-to for advice about anything and everything and told him what was going on. Finding a new job was out of the question, so the only thing left was to see what we needed to start the process of opening my first business.

There was so much to do. My aunt curated an inventory list of everything for sale, appraisal value of the item, and actual price. I helped her go through everything while figuring out what she would take with her, what I could afford to purchase, and what she would sell.

Dad and I then had to take the list to our banker to see what kind of loan I could get. Honestly, my confidence was not high in this whole situation. All I could do was take it step by step. After we left the bank, we had to speak with the owner of the little red building the salon was in and see if he would even rent to me.

I truly dreaded coming to work on Tuesday morning to find a lonely, quiet room, empty of all the things that made up the vibrant space I had planned on professionally surrounding myself with forever.

Not only was the building completely devoid of what used to make it Beauty and the Book, but it also meant I was starting from scratch.

Can anyone ever really be ready for something like this? Being thrown into business at such a young age with minimal training? I was not supposed to *own* a business. But there I was. Snapping out of my daze I realized there was no time to waste! I had bills to pay and I still needed to take care of what little clientele I had. I had to do this one day at a time.

After a little brainstorming, I came up with a business plan (when I look back at that "business plan" I laugh out loud). After giving my building a small face lift to really make it my own, Salon Rouge Spa & Boutique was born. It was just me providing as many services and I could, but it was perfect. Confidence was rising in me every day.

Just as I was getting into being a business owner and settling into my business, I discovered my husband was living a double life.

I never condone mixing home life and work life, but while going through this painful divorce, there were days where I could not control my tears. Just because I was crying uncontrollably didn't mean there weren't bills to pay. You cannot binge eat ice cream in your bed all day while watching *Legally Blonde* when you own a business. You just have to power through it like the badass you are!

It wasn't long before I welcomed a massage therapist and another hairdresser to the Salon Rouge Spa family. Up to this point, I still had not even thought of branding or expanding. I was not posting on Facebook regularly, and I didn't even have Instagram, YouTube, or any other social media. I should have been growing my online presence, creating a brand, and marketing my business, but I simply didn't know then what I know now, and I didn't know who to ask.

During the next several years I experienced one life-changing event after another. I met the love of my life unexpectedly in a restaurant and after two beautiful years of being together we decided to create a family of our own.

You know how they talk about a thing called pregnancy brain? Well, it's real and mine was concerning.

Coming back from maternity leave, I had the pleasure of welcoming a permanent makeup artist and her sister who was a nurse offering cosmetic injections.

That was when the lightbulb went off in my head: "I should open a spa!"

Why had I never considered going beyond hair and nail services in a little salon? Why had I never thought of all the possibilities of what this business could really be? I guess it was because I never thought someone like me would be capable of something like that.

We are capable of anything and we must never be the ones holding ourselves back!

I still had pregnancy brain and would forget everything, but I was not going to let that hold be back from expanding.

It was time to find a building, go back to the bank, and get a loan and begin construction.

The feeling of buying my own building and creating something that is truly mine was indescribable. It has been a long road from pregnancy and birth to construction and making the big move, but we did it. It is something to be proud of, especially considering I was only twenty-seven years old.

Just as we started planning our October grand opening, my husband and I found out my son, Tripp, had a Mesenchymal Hamartoma—a tumor in his liver.

At ten months old there was a ten-inch tumor in my son's liver. As we made the drive to Dallas over and over, my business was pushed to the side. Thank God for the amazing group of women I had at my side. I truly do not know what I would have done without them.

It was a hard situation to find myself in. The well-being of my child came first. At the same time, if I didn't pay my bills, I would be out of a job along with everyone else who worked with me. I will never forget how my team, as well as the rest of our community, came together for us.

You are never alone!

Tripp's surgery was scheduled for August 7, just two days before his first birthday.

Realizing he was recovering well, I was able to breathe again and dive right back in to focusing on my business and preparing for my October grand opening.

I was in a better headspace now where my business was concerned. I was really working on Facebook and using Facebook Live. I still didn't have Instagram and still had no conception of creating a brand. I was still extremely stressed trying to play catch up.

When my husband decided to run for County Judge my stress level, self-care, and business took another hit.

I was gone all the time helping him with his campaign. We were away until late at night and were not getting enough sleep. I was still working but I was so tired it was hard for me to pour my heart and soul into my work. On top of everything else, I was also on five community boards.

My attention was everywhere.

After my husband won his campaign, we dealt with some major backlash from a small group of people who were not happy with the outcome of his election. I was the main target during one particular situation and I really stopped taking care of myself. I stopped eating because I was sick to my stomach. I kept having nightmares, so I had huge dark circles under my eyes. I definitely was not drinking enough water. I was not laughing or acting like myself, and I was not able to perform my best work.

In hindsight, I learned a lot about how to handle situations and power through them. I am a better, stronger person for it. In my mind, I was recovering from the lack of self-care and severe stress, but in reality, the situation had done so much damage, I was having a hard time pulling myself back together.

This is where self-care comes in to play.

Taking care of yourself is NOT a luxury. How can you be a good business owner, parent, spouse, or anything if you aren't taking care of yourself? I learned this the hard way. You need to feel like the best version of yourself to do your best work.

Stress is a fascinating subject, and it can do some pretty incredible damage to you internally if you are not doing enough to decompress. Apparently, I was doing the bare minimum.

Now that it was summer and my cousin was out of school, we ran together every day. I had just purchased a new pair of running shoes and I was anxiously waiting for him to get to the salon so we could go run. I was finally starting to feel like my old self again and things were looking up.

We were doing interval running where we would sprint for a few minutes and power walk for one. We just broke off into a sprint and the next thing I knew I was waking up in the street behind the car wash in excruciating pain. I was terrified when I realized I could only move my upper body. I could barely speak through the sobs pouring out of me and I had no idea what happened.

There was severe damage to my right knee, left ankle, and I could not walk. My husband would have to take care of me and my child all by himself. I stand behind a chair for a living. How was I going to make money?

They ran test after test and basically it came down to everything I was going through and not allowing myself time to recover properly—mentally, physically, or emotionally. My vitamin levels were low, stress level was high, and I was simply not taking care of myself internally.

Lesson learned and LaFleur Couture Wellness Boutique was born.

I'll say it again: Self-care is a MUST!

The next year of my life I started getting my shit together. With the opening of my wellness boutique, it was time to crack down and really see where all of this could go.

I really needed to sit down and figure out how to run a store and work behind the chair at the same time. So, I came up with a great time management schedule that worked for both Salon Rouge Spa and LaFleur Couture Wellness Boutique. I created store hours, figured out the best ways to start marketing my business, and in what avenues to spend time networking.

I spent time studying like-minded brands, influencers, and bloggers to see how I can apply some of their strategies to my own business and pull it all together in a more professional and profitable way.

That's when it hit me: "I have a brand!"

It sounds so crazy, but like I said before, I was never in that mindset, so it never crossed my mind. I studied, networked, marketed through social media, created a posting schedule, started meditating, created a work schedule, got a budget together, found brands to work with, got off all the boards I was sitting on except for two, and dove into my work.

I could really see a huge difference once I changed my mindset and let me tell ya'll, I was on fire—my heart, soul, brain, creativity, EVERYTHING!

Then 2020 happened.

2020 was going to be my year! I was blossoming into this newfound businesswoman with my own brand. I had done a complete turnaround in running my business and I was overly excited to begin a new year with a new mindset.

Then we found out we had to shut down all salons and could only allow customers in boutiques to pick up pre-paid packages curbside or have them shipped to their homes. It would be extremely easy to let myself be discouraged, but I am not going to let myself fall into the trap of negativity. I am going to stay positive and productive.

It will give me time to work on my self-care, networking, and connections. I now have time to really study other like-minded people on social media and update my brand on my websites and social media accounts.

One thing I have always wanted to do with my business is start a web series. Why not take the time to do that now when I don't have anything else to do? I have never done anything like this before, but I am just going to jump in and try to help as many people become healthier and make sure they are taking care of themselves. I know I am not the only one who has gone through struggles.

One of my best friends has recommended I start meditating. The best time for me to have any kind of quiet time is at night when I lay down to go to sleep. Each night I meditate. I spray my pillow with lavender, take my lavender sleep gummies, apply my lavender moisture mask, lay on my pillow, and clear my mind. I get very still and quiet. This, of course, is after everyone else is asleep.

I repeat my positive affirmations over and over until I wake up the next morning. If you do not meditate, I highly recommend you try it. Having this change in mindset is transformative.

I can honestly say I am a completely different person than I was a year ago. I know what I have. I know where my businesses can take me. My path is clear, and I know I can succeed.

If you want to really progress, it starts with the right mindset.

It must come from within you.

ABOUT THE AUTHOR

BROOKLYNN BRADLEY-LAFLEUR

Brooklynn Bradley-LaFleur is the CEO and Founder of Brooklynn Three, the parent company of Salon Rouge Spa, LaFleur Couture Wellness Boutique, and This Beautiful Tripp Blog. She is also the host of the largest meeting and discussing book club in the world (The Pulpwood Queens Book Club) and has been featured on several entrepreneur podcasts.

Her mission is to help people transform their lives from the inside out by identifying internal and external complications they may be experiencing and connecting them with holistic based products and self-care services.

She hosts a "Self-Care Series" every Monday morning to help answer frequently asked questions and provide easy access to the benefits of different products and services to best serve her audience and their families. On Friday mornings she offers "LaFleur Couture Lives" to help people conveniently shop everything in the LaFleur Couture Wellness Boutique collection from the comfort of their own homes.

Invitation from the Author

Visit my website for a FREE wellness consultation to start living a healthier you:

www.Brooklynnthree.com

Company Name: Brooklynn Three

Website: Brooklynnthree.com

Facebook URL: https://www.facebook.com/brooklynnthree

Email: brooklynn@brooklynnthree.com

"There is nothing stronger than a broken woman who has rebuilt herself."

Shelley Biggs

It was January 1993, and my husband and I were standing in the center-stage front row of another network marketing event. Inner thoughts were harassing my mind and manipulating me to believe I didn't have what it takes to be an entrepreneur. Twenty-five hundred people were shouting and praising at the top of their lungs. Maybe they were instinctively experiencing the same state of mind I was in—feeling distorted and lured by words, spellbinding my soul and persuading me in, forcing me to feel like a failure if I don't join the craze.

The crowd was shouting, and the music was booming. It was deafening. We were standing directly in front of the presenters, waiting for the next guest speaker to come and speak about their version of the journey and what it takes to have genuine freedom as an entrepreneur. My head was spinning, and I was eight months pregnant at the time with our first child. I remember sweating and becoming very light-headed. My heart was racing with anxiety. The toxic air was filling my soul. My mind was buzzing with excitement. Maybe it was the stress of trying to measure up to the speakers, who had all "made it" to living a lifestyle of the rich and famous.

All I wanted to do was run out of the anxiety-ridden room. The only thing I remember was my husband asking me if I was okay. I blacked out right in front of the stage and fell to the ground. I don't even remember for how long.

This was the beginning of a journey I have been on—what I call the "hustling lifestyle." From then on, we were at meeting after meeting, staying up late, having had three babies, being exhausted from all the events ending at midnight.

I remember doing everything to gain success, going to marketing event after marketing event, living in hopeful expectation the next one would be "the one."

Honestly, the feeling gushing up inside me was fear of being left behind. I was driven to make it in life—having a sense of accomplishment was the greatest of all, and yet it left me feeling empty. Constantly battling in my mind, this driving spirit could not be healthy.

I know how the story goes because I lived it. I have lived in a world where you work hard twenty-four hours seven days a week, exhausted at the end of the day, put your head on the pillow and think to yourself, I did some work today. In reality, I was just running around trying to fill the void in my heart, trying to have a massive impact on those I serve. The relentless adrenaline junkie mindset screaming I must work hard and put in long days to live a successful life.

Wrong attitude!

How many times have I gone after my dreams, only to buy yet another course? This endless series of bright, shiny money-making objects only left me feeling without value, along with an empty wallet. How is it possible? I had to do a check on my thoughts. Was I buying into another money-making scam? Another shiny path only to dig myself deeper and deeper into debt? But I was doing what all the gurus said to do: Work hard, no sleep, go to all the events. They made me feel like a failure if I didn't show up. My mind was in high gear from all the hype, but internally I was endlessly falling down a black hole.

For twenty-eight years, I went down the high-adrenaline path. Back in the day as a stay-at-home mom, I was always rushing—rushing to get my kids off to school, rushing to get to all their games because the busier I am, the more productive I am. And on top of motherhood, I attended all sorts of self-development. I was buying into the mind game, always hustling down the road of entrepreneurship. It was exhausting.

Eventually I hit a wall. I was officially in a state of burnout.

For the first time in my life, I closed my laptop and didn't open it for three months. This was unheard of for someone like me. During the time of anti-hustling, I learned a valuable lesson. Time is valuable. What was I doing with my time, and how productive was I? Was I running in circles trying to figure it all out? Was I just buying another training desperately believing it would take me to the landing strip to launch my first product? And, by the way, asking myself, what *is* my product? How on earth will I get moving in a world that says I don't have a business if I relax, take weekends off, or go on a holiday with my family? And in the real world this is what most people are striving for—personal freedom.

Well, let me explain. I was "crushing it," but without making money. I was doing the groundwork and the tech work involved as an entrepreneur, but there was no money coming in, only money going out. I am someone who acts quickly, and yet all the actions took backfired on me. I felt self-doubt, low self-confidence, not worthy of being an entrepreneur and was going deeper into isolation by the day. Maybe I was impatient, but in reality, what I wanted was something that would take more time than I anticipated. I bought into the hype through persuasion. Sure, I was working on my business, but continually comparing myself to others and their success made me doubt myself into thinking I was not doing what it takes, and I needed to do *more*. If I wasn't where I wanted to be, then I must not have been working hard enough. My mind was falling into a pit, causing more chaos and crisis, only to leave me feeling hollow at the end. All the work I was doing felt useless. What I kept hearing from others was how if I haven't spent a certain amount of time in my business, I wasn't going to make it.

But eventually, I did learn how to use my time wisely and not just give in to the empty promises I kept hearing. The gurus were doing the *opposite* of what they said. I learned the hard way by giving in to their lies.

Take my advice—I can save you many years of heartache by not giving in. The independent spirit will say, "It must get done." But the inner spirit will say, "It isn't the real way." I advise following the inner voice and listen to the wisdom from the God-given spirit we are all born with. Follow it and never look back. Sometimes it takes us on paths we are not familiar with. Go with it because it is usually the right path.

I have been down every path you can imagine, from self-development events to marketing gatherings to whatever else suits your fancy. You can take the path where you pass out at eight months pregnant with your first child. I took that path twenty-eight years ago. I can't help but wonder if I was getting a message back then and didn't listen to my spirit about all the hustle and grinding that lay ahead on that path.

Does it look like there is a theme emerging here?

I have learned how going through all the hustle and bustle is not worth the agony and stress in the long run. Who was I trying to impress anyway? Is there an inner longing inside to be busy so others will think she must be on track because she works so hard?

There is a subtle message in the marketplace about hustling twenty-four hours, seven days a week. I was staying up late and felt like I was making it happen. In reality, there was only burnout at the end of that path.

I was a stay-at-home mom and had three daughters to raise, yet still went to every event that came up. If I didn't go to all the events, I felt like I wasn't measuring up as a mom. Society makes women feel like we can do it all. And often we do. Superwoman is her name, but the cost of mental health is the price you will pay. The feeling of being left behind is extremely powerful and I allowed it to take over my mind.

I let myself think I was on track and felt good about myself right up until suddenly everything I was doing came crashing down. A voice inside me said, "This is not what I have for you." It was a powerful voice. It stopped me in my tracks and made me feel like I was on a path of destruction. I thought I was doing the right things by attending all these events.

False hope had been lurking around me, and whatever stood in my way, I pushed it aside. But this voice knocked me off-track and changed everything. I was sobbing because I felt betrayed by all the hustle-till-you-make-it messages out there in the world.

I was overwhelmed by all the denial and betrayal. How did this happen to me? This question went around and around in my mind daily. I was constantly feeling disheartened and full of anxiety, thinking I would never make it as an entrepreneur. I got roped in, not once, not twice, but many times. And every time I bought into it, I would be full of hope and excitement only to be let down again by toxic marketing. I went down every rabbit hole hoping to find the answer while ignoring the void in my heart.

Being in denial seemed safe for me. After all, it was a false image I was trying to hide behind, not knowing which way to turn except to a glass of wine to soothe my hopeless soul. I felt off-track and caught in the hustle trap, falling deeper and deeper into despair, wondering which way was up, and ready to pack it all in, feeling like everything I tried wasn't working.

Then the world-wide pandemic happened, and one glass of wine at happy hour became two or three glasses of wine every day, and happy hour was at home. This clouded my mind with thoughts of giving up and looking to the wine to keep me satisfied.

The more significant challenges were my mental health and my sleeping habits. I would lie awake at night wondering how in the world I got myself into this mess. Anxiety was creeping in by the minute. An unfocused mind caused me to avoid the actual work I needed to do to get my business going. I hid behind the bottle of wine. Emotion-driven eating spiraled out of control. I was ready to give up and surrender it all. I began to really believe I was not cut out for the entrepreneurial world. I could not work twenty-four hours a day, seven days a week. Feeling like a fake and a fraud haunted me, as if I had been trying to be someone I'm not.

And then one day, out of the blue something extraordinary happened.

During the time of the pandemic, I was on my daily walk and stopped to just enjoy the moment, and immediately I heard a voice say, "Stay engaged." I felt the presence of what I think might have been an angel. It was full of strength and power, and it seemed to lift my spirit back to reality.

After this encounter, everything became clear in my mind. My thoughts were finally starting to line up. I felt a connection to the spirit inside me like never before. It was there all along, but I kept ignoring it and not listening to the still small voice. Suddenly, I finally felt ready for the battle I was facing. It was preparing me to take a stand and say no to the next hustling gig. My spirit started rising to the occasion, and I started believing I could make it happen. Something was rising inside me and saying, "You can do this." I had a deep desire to get moving on the right path.

I came to realize it was always my own thoughts standing in the way of my victory. The battle was going on *in my mind*. I was allowing the chatterbox of my thoughts to lead me astray and into a vicious cycle of buying into the next scheme while feeling I didn't have what it takes. I let my thoughts feed me toxic words—just give-up.

Finally, I had arrived at the place in my mind where I found victory, and my spirit was guiding me. I listened to my heart and believed the words: *I will make it*. I took a stand and stopped believing the lies in my mind. There were always two voices in my mind and had been listening to the wrong one! But now I was listening to the one leading me to rise and take a stand for what I believed in, to keep fighting even when things felt overwhelming.

These days, if I am feeling overwhelmed or stressed about a project, I back off and take a step back to analyze the situation and see if it fits in *my* schedule, not someone else's. Dangerous, toxic words have previously stopped me from moving forward, causing self-doubt and unbelief in a predictable pattern. I had to get up every day and fight the battle in my mind, beating back the poisonous environment of negativity.

All the odds were against me, and I felt like I would never make it in the world as an entrepreneur. I am sure others have also found themselves filled with self-doubt that clouds their minds, deceiving them into thinking they will never make it.

Now, however, I am in control of my mind and time. I am the one running my schedule. I can take the weekend off if I want without feeling guilty. I am not saying I don't believe in hard work. It does take work. But there is a difference between truly committing to doing something and just doing work so you can say you are working. If you listen to the voice telling you to work harder, work longer, then the result is inevitably crash and burn. I am a take-action kind of gal and don't like to sit on sidelines of indecision. Still, I have also come to realize all those quick yes answers got me into a heap of trouble in my mind, leaping into a hostile, toxic environment in my thought life.

Now I work shorter days, take days off when I want, and have more peace of mind. I feel more at ease because I decided to be me and say this is who I am—I am an anti-hustler.

However, there is a deeper reason for my anti-hustle attitude.

Finding my father dead from a heart condition in the garage when I was nineteen years old was not my idea of how life should turn out. My kids never had a chance to meet their grandfather. Rushing and hustling is what killed my dad at age fifty-six. He had his own construction business and worked long and hard but for what? An early grave?

The hustle lifestyle is the devil in disguise.

Call it whatever you like, but understand it is driven by fear in the deepest part of the soul. Unchecked, it leads to self-doubt and it made me even more insecure than I already was. It harassed my thought-life, causing me to get stuck in the hustle lifestyle. It made me think I could never measure up to all the entrepreneurs and it caused me to fall into a hellacious pit in my mind.

My challenge to you is this: Embrace the *anti-hustle* lifestyle!

Ask yourself what all the hustling has done for your mental health.

Three of my biggest successes in life call me mom. And that, my friend, is the greatest success any woman can have.

Embrace the anti-hustle lifestyle and win the battle in your mind today!

ABOUT THE AUTHOR

SHELLEY BIGGS

Shelley Biggs is a Certified Strategic Intervention Coach, author, and an AWAI Verified Direct Response Copywriter. By embracing her own faith, Shelley helps women empower their inner wisdom and achieve personal freedom by embracing the anti-hustle lifestyle to bring clarity into their lives.

Through years of studying human behavior, observing life situations, and her own personal experiences, Shelley has gained valuable insights into how to help women identify the obstacles holding them back. Believing there is a solution to every problem, her passion is to bring change and transformation to those with whom she works. Her philosophy is to connect first with their higher-self and then take positive actions to move forward. She believes we are not made to stay where we are at in life and encourages women to take healthy risks.

Shelley lives in Canada with her husband, Gregg, and their three daughters.

Invitation from the Author

Book a complimentary 30-minute Clarity Session with me to start living your most fulfilled life!

https://calendly.com/shelleybiggs-ent

Business Name: Shelley Biggs Coaching

Website: www.unmasktruth.com

Facebook URL: https://www.facebook.com/shelley.biggs.144/

Email: shelleybiggs.ent@gmail.com

Look for the third volume in this series:
She Rises for Tomorrow – Volume 3
Available soon!

Another great compilation of inspirational stories told by different entrepreneurial women from all across the world. Their shared stories will give you hope, motivation, and drive towards your future goals.

www.ingramcontent.com/pod-product-compliance
Lightning Source LLC
Chambersburg PA
CBHW070646160426
43194CB00009B/1594